One

One Score More:

THE SECOND 20 YEARS OF BURNING DECK

1982-2002

edited by Alison Bundy,
Keith & Rosmarie Waldrop

Burning Deck, Providence
2002

For financial help in publishing the volumes excerpted here we thank: the National Endowment for the Arts, RI State Council on the Arts, the Fund for Poetry, Taft Memorial Fund, the Cultural Services of the French Embassy, Pro Helvetia Foundation, Inter Nationes, and the following individuals: Craig Watson, Chris & Jeanne Longyear, Leonard Brink, Rachel Blau Duplessis, Harry Mathews, Eliot Weinberger, Kenneth Fain & Lisa Gim, Connie Coleman & Alan Powell, Christopher Middleton, Steve Evans, Patrick O'Shea, Shelby Matthews, Rena Rosenwasser, Roger Stoddard, Lawrence Fixel, Michael Gizzi, Romana Huk, Jay Scrivner, Karen Weiser.

For production help, particular thanks to Jennifer Martenson and Luisa Giugliano.

Burning Deck is the literature program of Anyart: Contemporary Arts Center, a tax-exempt (501c3), non-profit organization.

Cover by Keith Waldrop

© 2002 by Burning Deck
ISBN 1-886224-46-3

Distributors:
Small Press Distribution, 1341 Seventh St,. Berkeley CA 94710
1-800/869-7553; orders@spdbooks.org
Spectacular Diseases, c/o Paul Green, 83b London Rd., Peterborough, Cambs. PE2 9BS, England

Contents

• • •

•••

A Century in Two Decades was a selection of work from the first twenty years of Burning Deck, from our start in 1961 to 1981 — during which time we had moved from Ann Arbor to Durham, Connecticut, and from Durham to Providence. These moves were, of course, dictated by circumstances and from personal motives, but our small press had to tag along.

Without further relocation, it has, however, undergone several changes. Our own printing presses — often overworked in the old days — now rest in the basement, rarely used. Typesetting is electronic, the printing farmed out to professionals.

Two new series have appeared in our list. *Série d'écriture* was founded by the English press Spectacular Diseases to publish translations of contemporary French poetry. Edited from the beginning by Rosmarie Waldrop, it became a function of Burning Deck from volume 6 in 1990.

Since 1994, a parallel series, *Dichten* = [pronounced "Dichten equals"], presents translations of contemporary German poetry.

Longevity is not necessarily a blessing, but we have found, these two last decades, a somewhat wider response. In November 1991, Burning Deck was the focus of a weekend symposium at Fondation Royaumont in France and an exhibition at the Centre International de Poésie in Marseille. The Paris magazine *Prétexte*, in 1996, published a special issue on Burning Deck, translating selections from 14 Burning Deck books ("Carnet de traduction" No. 7).

And in our own country (we are not prophets) we were honored with exhibitions at Intersection in San Francisco, Milwaukee's wonderful bookstore Woodland Pattern, and Brown University Library.

Brown University's Graduate Writing Program held a three day festival, 19-21 March 2001, for Burning Deck's fortieth anniversary.

We would like to thank the people who created these occasions.

Prizes won by our authors include an American Book Award of the Before Columbus Foundation (*The Heat Bird* by Mei-mei Berssenbrugge, 1984), a San Francisco Poetry Center Award (*Paradise* by Ron Silliman, 1985), several Pushcart prizes (Dallas Wiebe, Barbara Einzig, Robert Creeley). Cole Swensen's *Numen* was a finalist for the PEN West Award (1996). Most recently, a poem from Barbara Guest's *Countess from Minneapolis* was selected for "Poetry in Motion" in Minneapolis (2001).

This Burning Deck anthology, marking our second score of years, reprints work from most of the books printed between 1981 and 2001, with the exception of a few which resist being excerpted: works by Barry Schwabsky, Gail Sher, Pat Smith, Joseph Simas, Gil Ott, Lew Daly, and Jennifer Martenson, for instance. Several authors we have published more than once (e.g., Craig Watson and Pascal Quignard) are represented by one entry each.

The presentation is chronological.

Materials are accumulating towards our third anthology.

K.& R.W.

One Score More

...

JOHN YAU

•   ••

LATE NIGHT MOVIES I

In a small underground laboratory the brain of a
movie actor is replaced by semi-precious stones,
each one thought to have once resided in heaven.

An archeologist realized the inside of an ancient
mask carried a picture of satin meant only for its
dead inhabitant. A nurse walked into a hospital
and knew something was missing.

In the afternoon, rain washed away all traces
of the railroad station. A crow hid its head
under its wing. A tourist sneezed twice and
wondered if there was any truth to the legend
inscribed over the doorway of the pharmacy.

Beware the opinions of a dead movie actor,
an empty hospital and a wounded crow on a rainy afternoon,
a missing brain and a train station built beside a river,
a nurse carrying a photograph of heaven.

In a small laboratory in heaven the semi-precious
thoughts of a movie actor are replaced by a brain.
The ancient mask realized the insides of the
archaeologist exuded a tincture of *Pisa*
meant only for its dead inhabitant.

Outside the train station the nurse wondered if
there was any truth to the legend inscribed
around the rims of her new tires. The brain
of the movie actor is carried by a tourist
from one day to the next.

In a small underground temple the wing of a crow
is replaced by semi-precious stones, each one
thought to have been a sneeze from heaven.

The nurse hid the hand of Orpheus under a painting
of a train statin, whose shadows reached the river
where all legends began. A doctor realized the
doorway of the pharmacy was missing. A woman
wondered why a picture of heaven had replaced
her tires.

The movie actor's only desire was to be seen
by the dead, to be fixed in the lining
of the clouds over their graves.

The archaeologist slept in a hospital with
as many windows as days in a year and wondered
if there was any truth to the legend inscribed
on the semi-precious stones the tourist carried
across the plaza in the afternoon rain.

At times, the nurse thought the only desires
were the ones without names.

The head of Orpheus floated down river, leaving
behind the hospital, where, as one version
of the legend claimed, the song would continue
forever in the hallways leading to the sea.

ANTHONY BARNETT

• • •

from: *A FOREST UTILIZATION FAMILY*

EXTRACTION

A loose   process   moving
                                                fuel
    from   place of growth to some
                    delivery
        or further   manufacture

confused   its   sense of pulling out by
force

FOREST UTILIZATION

                                    try
                                              delivery
to the consumer, of
                          every   art
        according to its   end

16

RAY RAGOSTA

••   •

THE CAPITALIZATION OF 'CLUE'

What we perceive is corpulent, well-dressed,
monocled, holds its middle against expansion.

From this, the avoidance, we infer a precept:
'at extremes lies the origin of design.'
(In other words, the big Clue,
capitalized here as it assaults the metaphysical.)

Hot on the Clue's trail,
we find the extraordinary
arising from the most unextraordinary.
(Yet there are no strange beasts:
neither bulls with brass hooves
nor creatures whose aromatic breath lures prey.)

Ordering eggs 'over light' it seems
we surpass our own illumination.

Remember the capitalization of 'Clue'?

We watch all this, ourselves,
from darkness.

DALLAS WIEBE

•   •   •

OBITUARY

William Weary called this evening, August 13, 1976, at about 6:30, collect, to tell me that my only sister, Grassgreen, was dead, that she had died at 4:32 A.M. in Bethel Hospital of a "coronation trombone" and that he was calling because Dirtbrown, her shitfaced husband, couldn't talk because he was out somewhere drunker than snot on a doorknob and he'd asked Weary to call and I couldn't hear much of what he was saying either because he's eighty-six now and mostly whispers because he's drunk most of the time too on Almaden Grenache Rose, which he can get because he's on Social Security, which pays him just enough to last one month of drinking if he drinks that wine, mixed half and half with water, out of a glass of ice cubes. I mostly said "What?" but did hear enough to know that it was up to me to do something with the body that was in the morgue at the hospital, cooled, unembalmed, unfeeling now and no longer remembering me and could no longer pick up that phone and call me, collect, here in Cincinnati because they lived in poverty, somnolent, broke, thinning out, withering up, dead still, in front of the TV set which I bought them eleven years ago while I was out demonstrating against wars, university presidents, the NRA, the cops, the prosecuting attorney, the Citizens for Decent Literature Under Law, parking lots, condominiums, automobiles, and teaching my classes for a salary that allowed me V-8 Juice, vitamin pills, melba toast, canned sockeye salmon, one bottle of Budweiser per day, one room with no windows, brown Bass Weejuns, Levi's and twenty dollars a week for Grassgreen and Dirtbrown to live on. I told Weary that I'd call the Lichgate Funeral Parlor in Newton and tell them what to do with Grassgreen's corpse, told him not to worry about it, that I'd pay for it, and to tell Dirtbrown to have a drink on me because I'd send him a dollar as soon as I could. William Weary also told me that I would have to write the obituary and send it to the *Evening Kansan Republican* and that I did and it'll only cost me a thirteen cent stamp.

"Grassgreen was born Agatha Theresa Seiltanzer on July 24, 1920, in Newton, Kansas, in Bethel Hospital at 3:30 A.M. She was the daughter of

Andrew Aaron Seiltanzer and Edwina Josephine Seiltanzer (née Mistwagen), now both deceased. Agatha Theresa attended Ferdinand Elementary School, Newton Junior High School and Newton Senior High School. Although she did not graduate from high school, leaving her studies at the age of sixteen because of financial exigencies, her teachers said that she was a very promising student. While in Junior High School, she participated in the concert band, playing the cymbals with great energy and concentration. She served as an usherette at the Junior High School production of "Ad Astra per Aspera" and it was noted that she made sure that each member of the audience got an uncrumpled copy of the program. Her diligence and concern also manifested itself when she was appointed to wash the volleyballs for her physical education class which she did carefully and faithfully in the shower. Before leaving the confines of formal learning, Agatha was much respected by her fellow students and she participated in many social events. She was known to her classmates as 'Ticky.'

"After leaving the halls of learning, Agatha Theresa spent her first year of unemployment productively by engaging in the formative education of her six year old brother, Skyblue. She guided him in his reading and writing and comforted him when their parents were away at the State Fair in Hutchinson, at the fireworks on the Fourth of July in Peabody, at the zoo in Wichita or listening to "The Messiah" in Lindsborg. Grassgreen's first fulltime job was as a sacker of potato chips in the McMannus Potato Chip factory. Here she worked diligently for a year and a half, humming, scooping up the potato chips in a card-board scoop, pouring them into the waxed bags, never breaking any, quickly weighing the bags and stapling them shut with a crisp snap. She eventually discovered that ten cents an hour was not an adequate compensation for her time and so she sought employment elsewhere. Mr. McMannus regretted her leaving his employment. He said that she was the best sacker he'd ever had and that he'd not once seen her eat a potato chip while on the job. Her next place of employment proved to be unfelicitous. Grassgreen's six weeks of waiting on tables at the Highway-Y Cafe was terminated when the State Board of Health determined that the cafe presented a health hazard to those who might partake of its nourishment. Subsequently, Agatha Theresa found happy employment at the Joblot Clothing Store as a clerk in the overalls department. She continued in this position until her marriage and when she left the Joblot Clothing Store the manager, John A. Stulpe, called affectionately

"Ten-fingers Jack" by Grassgreen, said that she refolded the overalls, especially the bib overalls, and put them back on the shelves better than any clerk the store had ever had.

"On June 24, 1941, she was married to Benjamin Paul Kitzler, an industrious farmer from west of Newton. After a two-day honeymoon in the Ozarks, the happy couple returned to their farm and took up the responsibilities of farm life. Their first and only child, La Donna Magdalene Kitzler, was born on March 2, 1942, at 2:15 A.M. in Bethel Hospital. However, their joy in parenthood was shattered when they learned, approximately two years after her birth, that La Donna Magdalene suffered from a birth induced deficiency. Agatha and Benjamin thus were forced to spend a great deal of effort and time in the care of their beloved daughter, even traveling as far as Wichita, Kansas, to seek out a cure for La Donna's difficulties. But they found no succor.

"Although both Agatha and Benjamin worked very hard in their agricultural pursuits, they found that five successive crop failures made it impossible to continue their profession. Therefore, they left their rural lives in 1965 and moved to a small house at 917 Chillblain Street in Newton, just one block away from where Grassgreen grew up, and took up their lives again despite a general aura of failure. Agatha Theresa was employed for a time as a waitress in the Chip and Dip restaurant until major surgery in 1969 forced her to retire. Benjamin Paul worked for short periods of time as a carpenter's helper, a sanitation worker for the city, a custodian at the Red Weeney Cafe, a railroad track maintenance worker and a landscape gardener. All of their situations of employment proved insufficient to maintain their existence. Eventually, a close and charitable relative became their benefactor, providing them with adequate financial and spiritual sustenance.

"Agatha Theresa Kitzler passed away on August 13, 1976, in Bethel Hospital. She is survived by her daughter, La Donna, aet. 34, now confined to the Kansas State Home for the Mentally Retarded in Zimmerdale, her husband, Benjamin Paul Kitzler, said to be incapacitated by alcoholism, and her beloved brother, now a highly respected Professor of English at the University of Cincinnati, Skyblue the Badass. Funeral arrangements will be made by the Lichgate Funeral Parlor of Newton and will be announced shortly."

And that's that. For a thirteen cent stamp. Except that I have remembered to remember. I have remembered to remember that Miss Kitty Carbuncle, my first grade teacher, read my name from the class roll on the first day of first grade and said, as I sat tall and straight on my green chair under the Wandering Jew, "You must be Grassgreen's brother. You look so much like her with your blond hair and your blue eyes. I just know you'll be a good student." And I was. Like Grassgreen. I learned to read about Dick, Spot, and Jane. So easily. It was the wonder of words and the sense leaping from the pages of the shredding, greasy little green and black books. And watched the science experiments: water evaporating from a jar lid to show that the sun took up water or spying on a cocoon until the moth emerged or watching one praying mantis eat another one. Ate my cooky at recess and walked home where my little, flabby mother made gravy to spread over bread and me loving every bite of that slop. And she, Grassgreen, bathing in the old zinc tub and me getting to bathe next in her water still warm and smelling of Ivory soap. The knothole in her bedroom door. The cigarette smoke drifting into my room so that I got up to see if the house were on fire. Ticky putting her arms around me and telling me how she loved me and what a fine young man I was. She helping me study, drilling me in reading and arithmetic until by the third grade I knew more than she did. With Dad and Mom beaming as I walked off to school to defeat everyone in the first, second, third, fourth, fifth and sixth grade in contests of addition, subtraction, multiplication and division. And me bringing home one perfect spelling paper after another until one day I misspelled "separate" and the whole neighborhood said, "See. He's not perfect." With Mom blushing and Dad frowning because the WPA and the CCC burned his ass and he walking around telling everyone that Roosevelt was a Jew.

While on vacation in the thick Newton Summers of our Youth, the heat gathered along the brick streets. The tar bubbled out from between the bricks and Grassgreen and I chewed it because we thought it would make our teeth white. Slow rise of black bubbles like the bubbles in the bread dough that stood on top of the stove and was covered by a towel. The rise so slow it couldn't be seen, but after an hour the difference was there. And the heat smelled of that tar as it gathered along the surface of the street and shimmered into the mirage of water just beyond the next alley. When rain came, the first few drops of water would slap down and leave tiny moon craters in the gutters full of dust. A sort of hissing arose as the drops plopped. As the rain gathered momentum, the first runoff was warm and smelled of the tar and the hot bricks. Then all was cold as the deluge fell. On our front porch, Ag and I shivered and looked into the dangling lightning. On our porch we drew up against the clapboards and trembled in the exploding thunder. Deep in the rainstorm we felt the wipe out that is peace. Ripping along our roofs, the heavy showers locked us in our shivering selves. The thin spray from the wind covered us with droplets of cold. The wind whipped our sodden hair. And we watched the cold refreshment that is the rain cleanse our world. When the sun broke out again, the leaves shone on the elms, the bricks of Nagol Street glistened, the tar bubbles froze unbroken, and we built mud dams in the gutters to preserve that fleet coolness for our shriveling feet. When the rains came in the night, we shrank under our covers and in the morning there would be broken nests and rubbery baby birds strewn about the backyard. The eyes of the blue-gray baby birds bulged over their scowling beaks and their bodies were naked except for a few strings of yellow fuzz.

The clothes on the washline measured as much as anything the growing up of Grassgreen. I remember first the frocks, the dresses with pleats in the skirts and puffed sleeves made of cotton cloth printed with white polka dots on yellow, red and white checks, green and white checks, red polka dots on white for Sundays. Hanging in the Spring breezes and drying beside Dad's long Big Mac overalls, beside my Mom's barrel-shaped corsets and beside my own tiny Levi's with their flies unbuttoned, pinned with two clothespins to the heavy wire along the sidewalk, jumping up and down as the line swung under its weighted, wet clothes, the fly open and the whole inside exposed to the prying sun. Then the dresses got tighter and darker, silk hose appeared, shining like deerskin and crumpled without a shaved leg in them. The underclothes went from white cotton with dark stains in the crotch to silk things that had rhinestones and little pink bows by the elastic around the tops and around the leg holes, transparent, the sun glistening off, while the brassieres got bigger and bigger, white to black, from white to dark red and icy greens. And the blouses with fewer and fewer buttons beside the B.V.D.'s and the holey Jockey shorts of my secretions. My own little bulges nothing beside the public advertisements of our mother's roundhouse bloomers and flour sack bras, my skyscraping Dad's shirts that almost touched the ground, swept over the iris under the washline while drying, nothing beside the glittering silk pennants from the hidden drawers of Bulshe's

Ready-To-Wear. Little shriveled, withered transparent balls of brilliant reds, greens, blues, blacks, hanging like sick caterpillars weaving themselves into cocoons on the heavy wire above the iris, beside the peonies, not far from the asparagus and the strawberries.

Grassgreen had several boyfriends before she married Dirtbrown. The first I remember, and the most memorable, was a tall, muscular man named Marcus Seligman. He was older than Grassgreen, about twenty-four, I think, and she was about sixteen. He was a farmer and a good one. He had inherited a large farm and was living on it and working the land by himself. Handsome, tall, strong. Wore a mustache, brown and full. Brown hair. Soft brown eyes. Gnarled hands. Always wore a tan work shirt and tan work pants. Either he washed the same pair over and over or else he had lots of those sets.

Once he gave me a dime. Once he gave me a piggy-back ride to get me out of his way. Once he caught me peeking in the bushes and took my pants off and swatted my bare ass. Later he apologized. Gave me a quarter. Rubbed my hair and I felt like hugging the man. He always smelled good too. Not of deodorants or soaps or lotions. Like a man who works hard, thinks little, bathes once a week and has a love that makes him have that odor of sweat and hair. I read once that good smells good. That saints often are detected by their odors. I never smelled a saint. But I remember the texture of his shirt, of his hard skin, his creamy smile, his oiled boots, his odor that I still associate with a long memory of one man.

Of a Saturday evening he'd come to town and he and Grassgreen would sit on the front porch in the swing. He'd drive his old green pickup truck to our old house on Nagol Street, park it, and pretty soon, while I lay in my room, I'd hear the squeaking of swing chains, the cracking and snapping of slats, the grinding of feet against the floor as they shifted around in various embraces. Say there was spirea. Say the iris was out. Say there were lots of mosquitoes and beetles. Say the bats dived in close and took insects right off the ear. Say Grassgreen giggled and snuggled. Say I heard Marcus murmur. Say they drove off for a Nehi grape soda or a Nehi cream soda. I never heard them return because I'd be asleep and then Ticky would get up at about 3:00 P.M. the next day, wander around sighing, eating lots of banana cream pie and chocolate cake.

Once Grassgreen and I drove out, she driving the old DeSoto, to his farm east of Newton. It was huge and flat. The house was old and unpainted. There were no trees around it. Marcus lived in one room and cooked in the kitchen. We went in briefly and then sat on an old horsehair stuffed sofa in a screened-in porch. He was covered with Evening in Paris. I sat alone, a chaperone of six. Then he went back to work. He drove the big Case tractor, the lugs flashing as they turned, the plow's four cutters, shears and moldboards sparkling as he roared away from his gas pump. That was the last we saw him. A neighbor found him three days later. His tractor had rolled over on top of him and he was crushed in the bottom of a gully. The man who found him said the corpse smelled worse than anything he'd ever smelled. At the funeral, the casket was not open. Grassgreen and I and one other woman attended the funeral. The minister, I remember, wore overalls and tennis shoes because he came in, for a few hours, from his own plowing to preach in order to preside over the burial of the dead muscle. We, the four of us, then followed the hearse out to Greenwood Cemetery in a black limousine, saw the casket lowered, threw clods of dirt onto the booming lid. As we left, the other lady, dressed in black with a thick black veil over her whole head, looked at Grassgreen and me for a while. She rode back to town in the hearse. Grassgreen and I walked back and she wept all the way. Mainly, I think, because she told me later, that she had no photo of him. We never saw the other lady again. We wouldn't have recognized her if we had. A few weeks after the funeral, Grassgreen began receiving Good Housekeeping in the mail. It was a birthday present from Marcus, posthumous.

I missed him for a long time. And maybe still do. He often appears in my V-8 dreams. I remember well that the last time we saw him, the time we drove out to his farm, that as he walked away to his Case tractor to return to plowing his wheat fields, he walked behind our wine DeSoto, stopped, waved to us and grinned, squatted with his back to the car, hooked his hands under the back bumper and lifted the back end of the car off the ground. When he dropped it, the car bounced around for a while and some gas sloshed out of the overflow tube beneath the gascap. On his way to his orange tractor he jumped into the air and kicked his heels together three times. Cavalierly waved his straw hat to us as he roared out to tear up the earth.

Grassgreen had another boyfriend, maybe more, I don't know, before she married Dirtbrown. Her other boyfriend was Oliver Winger, a town fellow and slick. Oliver wore rubber bands around his sleeves to hold up the baggy parts of the arms. He wore two-colored patent leather shoes, say, brown and white. Say, red and white. Say, black and white. Say, purple and white. He wore thin shiny white silk socks and purple garters to hold them up. His sailor straw hats always had red bands around them. He swaggered a lot and used toothpicks constantly. His black mustache was always neat; he shaved twice a day. Got his hair cut once a week by appointment. His vests were bright red or orange. Black bow ties and thick black belts. Sometimes yellow or blue suspenders, along with the belts. He drove a Model-A Ford coupe with a rumble seat in it. Tan canvas top, green body, red wire wheels. When he turned down from Broadway, he owned the gutters. When he rode up Nagol street to pick up Grassgreen, he was king of the bricks. When he stopped in front of our house, he passed out sticks of Dentyne. One night he taught me how to play a card game called "Fifty-two Pickup." When the first drive-in movie theater opened in Wichita, he took Grassgreen there for the first night. And she was the first woman in Newton to spend one whole date in the same car seat.

Oliver passed out of the life of Agatha Theresa when she was nineteen and he was twenty-three. He disappeared. No one ever knew where he went. His car, his garage, his house were all intact and nothing was out of order. He owed no money that anyone knew of. He had no known business even though he always had lots of money. If he had enemies they weren't from Newton. The longest anyone could remember him being gone from town was a week. And he went to Wichita about once a week to the zoo for three days. For many years his mother, Mrs. Celeste Winger, questioned the police and other people about the bodies found floating rotten in the rivers of the state. Questioned everyone about those skeletons found when digging sewer ditches. Questioned everyone about those corpses found in country ditches, in open sewers, in wheat fields, in wooden kegs, in steamer trunks at the railroad station, in abandoned barns, in dry wells, in weed patches, in the trunks of abandoned cars. She circulated his picture. Even passed out copies on the streets to everyone, mailed them to the police in lots of towns. If one of those skeletons was Oliver, it was not known. Silence and emptiness. Silence and absence. The bright red wire wheels and the rumble seat auctioned off and made into a hot rod. His clothes appearing now and then on Salvation Army indigents. Grassgreen with her Bible full of little notes which Oliver sent her and which she burned on the night before she got married to Ben Kitzler.

Grassgreen married Dirtbrown in 1941, a month before she was twenty-one. We had ice cream bars packed in dry ice and we played Picking Up Pawpaws on the yard of his farm where the reception was held. Where he came from I never knew. He was just there in his red Plymouth coupe. He with his Dick Tracy hat and Agatha with her Marlene Dietrich hairdo and hat and ready to end that great female daydream that runs from the beginning of menstruation to giving birth. She cried all during the ceremony and her white gown was streaked when she bawled her way into that coupe with the Campbell's tomato juice cans tied to the back bumper and "Just Married" written with soap on the trunk lid. Headed off to the Ozarks for their two-day honeymoon. I remember that I called out, as they pulled out of sight, "Good luck!" Grassgreen waved to me and that, I thought then, was the end of my comforting her in tornado and rain, in hail and snow, in cold and wind, in measles and mumps, in scarlet fever and chicken pox, in acne and cramps, in dead boyfriends.

Grassgreen gave birth to her daughter and only child, La Donna Magdalene, on March 2, 1942, who was premature and retarded. She is now thirty-four and still has the mind of a four year old. I pay for her care at the state hospital. On the day of her birth, I went out and worked hard cleaning out the rotten ensilage at the bottom of the silo. All day I stayed in that acidic juice in rubber boots and scooped out the rotten silage. At the end of the day I smelled bad. I went into town and sat out "Brother Rat" in the Regent Theater. People moved away from me. That night I slept in the barn. In the hay mow. Two years later we knew there was something wrong. Grassgreen called me in from the field one day and told me. I was plowing while Ben P. was out playing punchboards and getting drunk when I saw her standing in the gate through the hedge. I figured something bad had happened. But I finished my furrow and stopped the red Farmall, left the motor running to keep it from boiling over, and walked to her across the hard clods. I was covered with dust and she looked haggard. While I sipped warm, hard water from the wooden keg she asked me to come to the house for a while. I stopped the tractor. It began to boil in the heat. It was four o'clock and skin-cracking hot. She had been to the doctor with La

Donna. She sat in the kitchen and swatted at flies with a rolled up *Evening Kansan Republican* while she told me what the doctor had told her. It had to do with labor. It had to do with oxygen. Maybe it had to do with German measles. Or some such shit. While somewhere around me a red wall began to form. It rose and glowed. It seemed to be the rim of an eye that looked past me as if I weren't there. It was of the north. It was red and it got brighter. I felt it around me, on me, in me. I was afraid of it so I sat in the midst of a green valley, under willows by a blue stream. My dog, Magic, beside me. Cattle lay in the shade of the cottonwoods or stood in the deep mud along the creek. The sky seemed to spin away from me into endless shades of blue. Heat shivered across the plowed fields. Sweat ran down my face and left tracks in the dust. Grassgreen talked on about birth damage. I looked down the front of her print dress, saw sweat trickling down between her breasts. We drank hot coffee. The green grass was cool to my touch. The creek tingled in the soft light of a Spring sun. From the other end of the woods came the sound of a bird-man singing. He appeared. Dressed all in red and yellow feathers, he carried a panpipe, a glockenspiel and some cages made from sticks. He stopped and shared my ham salad sandwich with me. Told me that the mockingbirds were eloping with downy woodpeckers. Told me that the scissor-tailed fly-catcher edited the local newspaper. Told me that the meadow lark loved snuff. We talked on into the darkness. As the sun set, the red wall stood over us in red threat. We huddled together among the roots of a fallen elm. Red cold fixed our bones. Hopefully some training could be done and she would be all right. The doctor thought that probably sometime she would have to go to a home. When La Donna whimpered from the bedroom, Agatha wept and asked me to go and change her. La Donna's toes touched and completed the circle of her legs. Her fiddlestick teeth scraped at her lips and slobber ran down her neck. When I went back into the field to plow, it was evening. The sun was setting. The red wall was rising higher. I clawed at the earth with my plowshares. I laid over the soil. I shivered in the first winds of darkness.

My first horse of my very own was a gelding named Billie. Dirtbrown bought him at a sale because he wanted the bridle and saddle that went with the small horse. I worked for Dirtbrown for two weeks; my pay was the horse. Billie was useless, except to me, and he was worth all that work because he had been a polo pony and had grace and control. When I rode him I had to be careful not to fall since he turned so quickly. The first time I rode him I did hit the dust, but he knew not to bolt. I curried him and fed him out on Dirtbrown's farm. Watered him and watched him when he was in the pasture while I was out in the field. Loved him and rode him. Petted him and trimmed him. For six weeks. Then he died. A truck came for him and took him away with those other corpses, stiff bodies piled in a truck with their legs akimbo in the air. When I felt sick about it all, I'd think of those mornings when I would get up at dawn, saddle up Billie and pound out on those vast, empty country roads. Before the blistering heat of the day. Before chores and labor. Before an accursed world fell down over my eyes. Before Grassgreen's gritty, greasy breakfasts. Feet up and proud. Dancing along the hedgerows where the brown thrashers flew in and seemed to come apart as they went into the underbrush. Prancing along while skunks and 'possums cleaned up the carrion they had worked on most of the night. Raccoons slipping into their hollow trees. Birds awake and squabbling for the first bites of the day. Maybe a coyote loping. The air cool and clear before the wind might kick up and strip the land of its gentility. The leather in the saddle squeaking. The skin along Billie's neck quivering with every pat. And the gentle hoofs clicking in the first light of day. I, riding out into that world, a prince, made so by my fine horse. I jiggling and Billie his head up would come to the castle where the flags waved and the trumpets warmed up the breezes. Came to the castle, crossed the drumming drawbridge, clattered into the cobblestone courtyard where she waited with her long yellow hair for us to take her away. Sure and easy, we came and we took.

Our father stood 6'8" or so. Weighed about 165. His head often hit the tops of doorways and he suffered all his life from back trouble. When he died at the age of fifty-four (born 1900), he couldn't lift a bucket of water. In fact, there were times when someone, usually me, had to lift a glass of water to his lips so that he could drink standing up. I'd stand on a chair, even when I was full grown, and slowly tip the glass across his god-awful breath. If I poured too fast, he punched me in the stomach by swinging his arms sideways like the sidearm delivery of certain baseball pitchers. Somehow he could hit me in the pit of the stomach. When he milked a cow, he hunched on the stool, gripped the bucket with his knees and cursed with every jerk of his hand because of the pain that frittered out from his spine. He had to be helped up from the milking stool. So that sometimes when he was sitting there and a cow started pissing and the piss was washing over him and he was shouting for my help and he couldn't get up, I'd think, "Take that, you son-of-a-bitch," while I sidled over to him to get out of range of the fire hoses of our watery cows. Sometimes, while his legs and lap soaked up the splatter, I would waltz up, deadpan, help him to a stoop, kick the stool out from under him and then let him drop into a pile of cowshit. Actually he was too heavy for me to hold and often, if I was lucky, one of the cows would kick him while he was down.

Our mother, Edwina, was the happy one and I'm sure I got my joy and good will from her. She used to sing all the time — barroom songs, hymns, old favorites, popular songs, anything. I remember how she'd be scrubbing on a washboard and singing "I Come to the Garden Alone." She was happy, short and fat. One of the reasons I had to water my father was that my mother was too short to do it even if she stood on a chair. She must have been only about four feet tall. She had long blond hair that never faded. Her cheeks hung like draperies over her jaw. Her legs looked like they had dropsiding on them made out of skin. Her knees and ankles made one post with undulant wrinkles around it. When she walked, the fat jigged up and down. Trembled like sound waves through science films. She procreated twice, me and Grassgreen. Apart from that she washed clothes, cooked, went to church, sang and died a horrible death. When she got breast cancer, the doctors removed what they thought were her breasts among all that adipose. She screamed into the grave.

Our father died on December 21, 1954, when he was fifty-four and I was twenty-four and sipping beer in Metzger's in Ann Arbor. Mom called, collect, and told me that he was dead and I got on the late train to Chicago and caught the Chief out the next morning. When I got to Newton, my mother said he screamed for a week before he was neutralized and finally died in some kind of unconsciousness. His body was yellow in the satin-lined casket. His cheeks stuck to his jaws. His lips were cracked and you could see where something had been wiped into the cracks to keep the embalming juice in. His hair seemed brittle, like small twigs in Winter. The sermon was about the comforts of heaven. While that poor backbrained corpse lay there like a cheap doll in the five-and-dime of eternity, with his knees drawn up because the casket was too short, not even comfortable in death, his back angled to one side while old Mr. Presbyterian comforted the afflicted, whoever that was, by recounting the afflictions of others, especially Christ. You'd have thought that all Christ ever did was suffer. After all, he did live thirty-three years and spent only one day of those thirty-three years on the cross. I know he spent some time in the desert, but that was probably good for him. He probably lost a little weight, got his cholesterol back in line, flattened out his tummy a bit, toned up his muscles, exercised a lot, jogged and had, except for the cuisine, a pretty interesting time of it all. Out there with all those wonderful desert flowers and animals; lizards, wild sheep, jackals, bees, locusts, blossoms in crevices, cactuses, wind-rubbed stones. After which, one day of suffocating. My Dad took it for a month, at least. Not to mention what he suffered before he went into the hospital. And would not rise from the dead and no way ascend into heaven.

When we went to the graveside and dropped that white satin-lined casket down into that clean hole, it was bitterly cold. The wind slid across the prairies like a wild cat, belly to the ground and eyes fixed neurotically ahead. Our teeth ached under the thin overcast. Our feet became numb. When it came time for the ashes to ashes and dust to dust bit, there was plenty of dust — in the air. Cold dust it was, clipping us on the north wind like pellets. When it came time to toss in the clods, we couldn't. They were frozen together and so we didn't get to hear that great empty thump when dirt falls on a gray, brushed velour casket. We didn't get to hear that minor thud that foreruns the last trumpet. We didn't get to hear the galloping clods across the wooden lid, a galloping not too far off from those inevitable horsemen. Final prayer. Then we sang his favorite of the "Begräbnisslieder," in German and with that tune that is light and happy like a child's tune, like a game tune, like a child's joke about pooping and peeing. There, in that blistering wind, singing without books because we'd been there so many times before, our voices, lost in the wind, whined out that message that none of us ever believes. I wanted my money back. And I couldn't figure out why in the hell I ever paid for it all in the first place.

Our mother, born January 6, 1900, died on February 14, 1961 when she was sixty-one and I was thirty-one and sipping Heileman Old Style at the Badger Bar in Madison, Wisconsin. Agatha called me that night, collect. I was logged with beer and didn't get things quite straight. But I did get on a late bus and headed for Chicago and in the morning caught the Chief west to Newton. Out over all those intersecting tracks, black drawbridges, along the canal cut in solid limestone, past mountains of coal, past the huge limestone quarry, through the waste land to Joliet, and then out past pinkish-purple slag heaps, past strip mines now vaguely outlined under weeds and bushes, through the dull center of the U.S.A., over the Mississippi River on that squatting bridge to Ft. Madison, into the long jaunt across the prairies of Missouri and the soaring crossing of its river, for the dull wait at Kansas City and then into the flats of Kansas until the crosstracks and Peabody told me that Newton was just ahead. Walton whipped by. Then into that old town, Newton, with the other passengers all saying, "Why we stopping in this dump?"

No one met me — it was 8:34 P.M. — at the train so I walked out to the cracker box house on Nagol Street. Stepped once more on those splintering boards of the old porch, now seemingly smaller than it once was. The old swing gone. The house chipped and flaking. The porch falling. The elms all gone from around the empty house because of Dutch elm disease. Nagol Street's bricks now covered with asphalt. The deep curbings barely visible. Arrived home and walked into a nauseating recollection of youth to watch Grassgreen weep into her forty-first year while we carried our flabby Mom, lying in white satin, into and out of the church on First Street, hauled her out to Greenwood Cemetery, dumped her and her black, brushed velour casket and came home with cracked foreheads. Again the cold primed us for pneumonia while we got rid of her. Agatha told me about Mom's suffering. She sang a lot when I was her son but she shut up when they chopped off her chest and dropped her into that rank loam out of which comes the great wheat of Kansas. I stayed for a few days with Agatha and Ben out on their dead farm, trying to forget the bland sermons of the poor in spirit, trying to forget the screams of the meek, trying to forget the rewards of the righteous, trying to undo the confusion in the deaths of the merciful, trying to negotiate — I paid for it all, cash — the end of the peacemakers, trying to rejoice and be exceeding glad for the reward in heaven (Who'd pay for my funeral?), trying to outdo the revilings, persecutions and all manner of evil sayings falsely delivered against me that I was a smartass and stingy.

The last time I saw Agatha Theresa was in May of 1969. She called me, collect, to tell me that she'd had a hysterectomy and that, weeping, she wanted to see me again. And then it was the James Whitcomb Riley

31

to Chicago and west on Amtrak to Newton, the old trip, the constant ride, down into the old plains where I saw that she had not aged well. Where she told me how she hated the farm and was glad to be back in town. Her face was cracked. Her lovely blond hair was matted, graying and thinning. Her hands were knobby. Her lips pale. Her eyes were puffed and almost shut. We talked a while and she told me how tough menopause had been for her, how the pain was from the operation, showed me the sawblade livid scar and told me how she always wanted a son. She thanked me for the television set I'd bought them in 1965 when they left the farm for good. How they liked to sit on a long Winter evening, the wind racking their little house, and watch anything. Their only problem being that the TV antenna blew down often. Or, of a long, hot summer afternoon, the set on for "Edge of Night," "As the World Turns," or "Dark Shadows." And I didn't begrudge them their diversion. It might delay suicide or insanity. The tube filled up their thoughts and, maybe, prevented her from missing a son all the time, a whole son. They were broke, could hardly pay their rent, and I realized they'd die in poverty and I decided then and there to start saving money for their funerals. Grassgreen told me how La Donna Magdalene still sat in her hospital room and gurgled, then twenty-seven years old, played with her full breasts, gnawed at her lips and repeated endlessly, "Flies and worms. Flies and worms."

I turned back then to that red wall around that glowing green eye with the thick, black lens and saw the darkness on the face of the earth and on the face of the waters. Saw the cold sunlight and that leaves and grass are but dust. Saw the vast desolation of the ending of it all. Saw and knew our stupid faith in words. That we can say anything of any significance. That we think our sentences mean something. That we believe that syntax orders our world. Saw the idiot dogmas of metaphors, literary allusions, plots, paraphrases, questions and answers. Catechisms, bibles, history books, biographies, encyclopedias, dictionaries. Saw and knew the folly of learning, of causes, of governments, churches, poetry, plays, fiction. Saw in the layers of earth, the worms shrivel. Under the broken trees, carpets of dead birds. On the farms, plows rusting and seeds drying. Cows and horses peeling off in the deadly, level winds. Saw and heard the silence after laughter. The emptiness after the grunting and squealing. The breaking of worlds where the grand bull roared, where the grand cock crowed, where the gross boar slobbered. Saw waves of dead fish rise against the continents. Saw morbid whales roll aimlessly through the waves. Saw thick oil cover the creatures of the deep and clouds of poison folding up our cities. Saw the gutters full of rotting children who fell on their way to get an education. I saw the bright and shining morning star break and there was no more.

At 7:34 p.m. I picked up the phone and put in a call, collect, to the Lichgate Funeral Home in Newton. When Jim Bob Feigling accepted the call, I told him to haul Agatha's body to Wichita and get it cremated. He asked what he should do with the cremains and I told him to put them in a suitable container and deliver them to Ben Kitzler at 917 Chillblain Street. Tomorrow morning, Agatha Theresa will be burned into five and one half pounds of ashes. And the next day I'll get the bill.

TOM AHERN

• • •

POPEYE IN THE 19TH CENTURY

Popeye writes only for the ledger. Popeye wasn't mad. Wimpy didn't eat too much. Olive Oyl never trembled. Bluto spontaneously combusted. *A fact, and Dear Reader. Faithful representing of commonplace things furnishes the raw material of moral sentiment. Only water, said Charlie Plimpton, was fit to penetrate unfelt into the subtlest tissues, and without causing the slightest jar, to flow among the finest, most sensitive and most hair-like vessels. Popeye growed fond of extravagant landscapes buried beneath familiar hills. He and others traded things and when necessary, defended their sentiments with zeal every few years. As he sat by the fire, Popeye wondered if marrying he would encounter a shrew, if marrying he would discover his wife dead some brilliant day upon his return, if marrying, his children would predecease him. His slippers edged toward the fire, the dog snarled. Popeye's feet leaped high, and the fire ran through his home, of cynical purpose and yet welcoming salvation, deprived now of the bracing companionship of this furthering cartoon.

UNBRUISED

The lamps have been left burning in a fish, while wars damage former roles. Our boat slams the waves, eventually to dock in the Philippines.

The boat's bow dents the fish. Bulbs burst and the fish darkens. Now bruised.

THE RUBBER KNIGHT

A soul warmed in gutta-percha.
    Dreaded, for untrue.

POPEYE'S LAST WORDS

His endeavors were disagreements, and the lustre that sponged
his fat heirs, and his long tapering strokes capped in flippant pie
hats, fin, the end.

TITLED

In the green meadow stood a cow. Did I say it was blush?
In the damp meadow stood a cow. Did I say it was blush?
In the pearled meadow stood a cow. Did I say it was blush?
In the fallen meadow stood a cow. Did I say it was blush?
In the lush meadow stood a cow. Did I say it was blush?
In the navy meadow stood a cow. Did I say it was blush?
In the navy meadow stood a cow. Did I say it was lost?
In the navy meadow stood a cow. Did I say it was black?
In the navy meadow stood a cow. Did I say it was white?
In the navy meadow stood a cow. Did I say it was tan?
In the navy meadow stood a cow. Did I say it was grey?
In the navy meadow stood a cow. Did I say it was slate?
In the slate meadow stood a cow. Did I say it was someone else's?
In the slate meadow stood a cow. Did I say it was white?
In the slate meadow stood a cow. Did I say it was tan?
In the slate meadow stood a cow. Tom Ahern?

MEI-MEI BERSSENBRUGGE

•   • •

THE HEAT BIRD

A critic objects to their "misterian" qualities
I look it up and don't find it, which must relate
to the mystères in religions. Stepping
across stones in the river which cover
my sound, I startle a big bird who must circle
the meadow to gain height. There is a din
of big wings. A crow loops over and over
me. I can see many feathers gone from its wing
by sky filling in, but it's not the big bird
I walk into the meadow to find what I've already called
an eagle to myself. At first you just notice a heap
like some old asphalt and white stones dumped

———

There is a curving belly. The cow's head is away from me
Its corpse is too new to smell, but as an explanation
hasn't identified my bird. Twice I am not sure if light wings
between some bushes are not light through crow feathers
but then I really see the expansive back swoop down
and circle up to another cottonwood and light
It's a buzzard with a little red head. You say
that's good. They're not so scarce anymore. It should
have been more afraid of me

Fresh wind blows the other way at dawn, so
I'm free to wonder at the kind of charge such a mass
of death might put on the air, which is sometimes clear
with yellow finches and butterflies. That poor heap
is all sleeping meat by design with little affect
I decide in a supermarket, whose sole mystère is
an evocative creak in a wheel. Not unlike a dead stinkbug
on the path, but unlike a little snake I pass over
All night I pictured its bones for a small box of mine
Today I remembered, on my last night you wanted to
linger after the concert, drinking with other couples,
like a delicate dragonfly

———

And I can't predict your trauma. Potent and careless
as radiation here, which we call careless, because
we don't suspect anything. Then future form is in doubt
Like a critic I thought form was an equilibrium
which progressed by momentum from some original reduction
of fear to the horizon. But my son's thigh bones
are too long. I seduced myself. I thought
I'll give it a little fish for the unexpected. Its paw
moved. My back-bones are sparking mica on sand
now, that carried messages up and down

Glass that melted in the last eruption of the
Valle Grande has cooled, and you can just run
among wild iris on a slope, or fireweed in the fall
Its former violence *is* the landscape, as far as
Oklahoma. Its ontogeny as a thin place scrambles
the plane's radio, repeating the pre-radio dream
At any time, they all tell us, to think of eruption
as a tardy arrival into present form, the temperate crystal
I still see brightness below as night anger, not
because of violence, but its continuousness with the past
while airy light on the plain is merciful and diffuse
that glints on radium pools. I wanted to learn how
to dance last year. I thought your daughter might teach me

———

She did a pretty good job at elucidating something
she didn't understand and had no interest in
out of duty. She has evoked a yen for dance. Any
beat with wind through it. In an apricot tree
were many large birds, and an eagle that takes off
as if tumbling down before catching its lift. I thought
it was flight that rumpled the collar down like a broken neck
but then as it climbed, it resembled a man in eagle dress
whose feathers ruffle back because of firm feet
stamping the ground in wind. The other birds discreetly
passed their minutes with old drummers of stamina
but eagles entered swept ground oblivious to other drummers
making streams of rhythm in the repetitions
until pretty soon some of the other ladies' white feet
moved to them, too, bound thickly around the ankles
so their little claws look especially small

Where I saw their fine cross-hatch was competition
not air moving through air, or weather
though the water balloon she tried to dodge
as it wobbled this way and that like big buttocks
before breaking on her shoulder *was* rain. The rain
is not important. It rains, not very often
but regularly. If I am far from you isn't the current
of missed events between us an invention of potency
like a summer storm at night, or when I see you
A throw of food and household goods from the roof
to all of us became a meteor shower across fixed stars
In their parallel rain I can't judge each gift's distance

———

They took me to the little town where they were
working, because I asked them to take me. To my left
was an old porch with long roof boards going away
from me, on 2 x 8 rafters perpendicular to them
and the falling down house. The light was descending
to my right. Narrow cracks between the boards cast
a rain of parallel bright lines across the rafters
which seemed precise and gay in the ghost town
They were outside its time, though with each change in sun
they changed a little in angle and length, systematically
They were outside the carnage of my collaborative seductions
When I touch your skin, or hear singers in the dark, I get
so electric, it must be the whole dam of my absence pushing
I think, which might finally flow through its proper canyons
leaving the big floor emptied of sea, empty again
where there used to be no lights after dark

I looked to my right. Though sun wasn't yet behind
them, it was bright near each tree on the ridge
where they are single, because there can only
be one on the top of a ridge. These were precise
too, but on a closer edge outside time, being botanical
I mix outside time and passing time, across
which suspends a net of our distance, or map
in veering scale, that oils sinuous ligaments
or dissolves them into a clear liquid of disparates
that cannot be cleaned. Its water glows like wing bars
and remains red and flat in its pools. On the way
to that town there were green waist-high meters on the plain
There was a sharp, yellow dashed line on the blacktop
In rain it remains sharp, but its dimension below the road
softens and lengthens through aquifers. The eagles'
wingbones began to stretch open with practicing, so
luminous space in their wings showed against the sky
giving each a great delicacy in turns

———

Prosaic magpies arrive about the time ribs begin
to show a beautiful scaffolding over its volume
where the organs were. The buzzard now brings to mind
a defunct windmill with a wheel hub, but no blades. The eagle's
descending back still bears, after enough time has passed
when the event is articulate, and I know its configuration
is not mixed, or our mingling, or the "intent" of a dance
If a bright clearing will form suddenly, we will
already know of it

NANCY CONDEE

•°   •

MRS. CHARLES SANDERS PEIRCE,
or THE SOLUTION TO THE UNIVERSE

In the course of his life, her husband determined with unprecedented precision the shape of the Milky Way, refined the calculations of the earth's ellipticity, computed the meter's length in terms of the wavelength of light, could write with either hand, in fact, could write a question with one hand while writing the answer with the other, did book reviews, lectured on logic, and wrote science definitions.

She added a third floor to their house. This was done so that she would have a place to hold the commemorative ball after her husband solved the riddle of the universe. Here, she thought, despite the vastness of the universe with all its galaxies and so forth, on a planet the size of a drawing pin, on the third floor of a house named Arisbe in Milford, Pennsylvania, hopefully in the spring, men and women in their finest would dance to celebrate the day when the universe was at last understood; and William James and his wife, the earthographers and astronomers from the Coast and Geodetic Survey, and the President of Johns Hopkins University himself would finally realize with whom they were dealing. And even the universe, that old sphinx, would ask itself how it could have so underestimated the resourcefulness of Charles Peirce and would feel a twinge of regret that it had made the riddle so easy.

ROBERT COOVER

GETTING TO WICHITA

So the driver eases off the interstate up the exit ramp and on into a filling
    station spies a fat mechanic in greasy green overalls purple baseball
    cap rolls the window down hey buddy
the mechanic stares at him dully chewing a thick wad a smear of grease
    across his cheek monkeywrench in his hip pocket cuffs rolled knees
    blackened
how far's it to Wichita?
the mechanic watches him awhile then spits tucks a ballpoint behind his
    sunburnt ear shuffles away toward a battered Dodge on three wheels
    and a jack
hey the driver hollers leaning on the horn
hey I'm talking to you mister
the mechanic turns back slowly squinting in the sunlight
I asked you
lifts the monkey wrench from his hip pocket tips his cap back with it
how far's it to Wichita?
where the wheel turns says the mechanic flatly the void gnashes its teeth
howzat?
the mechanic gazes at him vacantly picking at a pimple on his fat cheek
listen pal all I wanna know is can I get there before six?
the mechanic squeezes the pimple wipes it absently with a greasy sleeve
it is beyond calculation beyond analogy he says standing there on the
    oilstreaked concrete in his overalls working his thick jaws mechanically
    around the rosy wad of gum scratching his ass with the monkey-
    wrench
those who seek to burn the sky with a torch end in tiring themselves out
    therefore cease from measuring heaven with a tiny piece of
awright awright snaps the driver irritably wheeling around to the pumps
    with a squeal of his tires
fill er up goddamn it
sure mister says the mechanic pocketing his monkeywrench coming over
he leans down to the window smiles pops his pink gum
regular or premium?

THE FALLGUY'S FAITH

Falling from favor, or grace, some high artifice, down he dropped like a discredited predicate through what he called space (sometimes he called it time) and with an earsplitting crack splattered the base earth with his vital attributes. Oh, I've had a great fall, he thought as he lay there, numb with terror, trying desperately to pull himself together again. This time (or space) I've really done it! He had fallen before of course: short of expectations, into bad habits, out with his friends, upon evil days, foul of the law, in and out of love, down in the dumps — indeed, as though egged on by some malevolent metaphor generated by his own condition, he had always been falling, had he not? — but this was the most terrible fall of all. It was like the very fall of pride, of stars, of Babylon, of cradles and curtains and angels and rain, like the dread fall of silence, of sparrows, like the fall of doom. It was, in a word, as he knew now, surrendering to the verb of all flesh, the last fall (his last anyway: as for the chips, he sighed, releasing them, let them fall where they may) — yet why was it, he wanted to know, why was it that everything that had happened to him had seemed to have happened in language? Even this! Almost as though, without words for it, it might not have happened at all! Had he been nothing more, after all was said and done, than a paraphrastic curiosity, an idle trope, within some vast syntactical flaw of existence? Had he fallen, he worried as he closed his eyes for the last time and consigned his name to history (may it take it or leave it), his juices to the soil (was it soil?), merely to have it said he had fallen? Ah! tears tumbled down his cheeks, damply echoing thereby the greater fall, now so ancient that he himself was beginning to forget it (a farther fall perhaps than all the rest, this forgetting: a fall as it were within a fall), and it came to him in these fading moments that it could even be said that, born to fall, he had perhaps fallen simply to be born (birth being less than it was cracked up to be, to coin a phrase!) Yes, yes, it could be said, what can not be said, but he didn't quite believe it, didn't quite believe either that accidence held the world together. No, if he had faith in one thing, this fallguy (he came to this now), it was this: in the beginning was the gesture, and that gesture was: he opened his mouth to say it aloud (to prove some point or other?), but too late — his face cracked into a crooked smile and the words died on his lips. . .

MICHAEL GIZZI

•• •

from: *SPECIES OF INTOXICATION*

Versailles
—Galérie des Glaces

Revenge the attitude I need never attend. Not too

Is dusk and soft foliaceous labials, oping o's tween movin'
leaves trees. In lights one's reach is light, like. Lamped stare
stares in.

Lucidities at trancin' moment. One caresses sliding over
habits only shimmer's flexion, texture risk paralysis, both
        meanings winkin', one t'other.

Clairvoyant crystal palpitating concavity. Mirror's addict
moment.

Thought in her first arms convinced of wantin' everything
the eye's self

Deers out a long skirt. not neural debris

Drink only to excess

Detox with women   Or what you like, the surface of
her leaf wavy like the surface of the sea. A loin perhaps, or
lupin — 'long purples' called *orchis mas* but liberal shepherds
give a grosser name!

Is not the root a privy part, happy with little inward
leafcakes, trickle escapin' from a corner of delight?

Of course androgyny is one inflection of paradise — the
feathers one hasn't, the other half has. Only,

mind your head when risin'

CHRISTOPHER MIDDLETON

from: *WODEN DOG*

Silva smoak of pine
Burn chill
Woden dog shivver
Owl not heard

Lightslice fix to floor
Think dead
Woden dog like ice
In his box owl not heard

Owl hoot rainbow
Out of owl eyes
Owl hoot rainbow wonder
Dog not see dog bark at ghost

Owl not heard
Dog munch heap white aple
Not feel snow as owl bountie
Not smell snow rainbow

Woden dog eat heap
Aple up
Pip corn all cold aple meat
Not see owl

Not see some owl eyes
Not hear
How pips look sound yum yum
Crunch owl eyes aple up

Dog wine in boxn stay putn scoff
Woden dog alltime scoff
Woden dog shut in wod
Not smell sweet pine

Woden dog not smell wind song
Burn swingin low
Swingin in pine wod
Owl not hoot fur him in pine log

Owl not hear in dog box
He woden dog
Snow owl hoot that rainbow now
Now hootn touch dog heart

W. D. SNODGRASS

from: *SIX MINNESINGER SONGS*

Wizlaw von Rügen: "Only Love"

Only Love and Love's longing fills my singing;
To myself, were I bringing
Pleasures my own will might gain
So my days might pass relieved of sadness,
I could bring others gladness,
Rising to a higher strain.
I'd forswear these lovesick songs of yearning,
All men's praises earning
Evermore, and to old age gladly turning
Freed of every pain.

Yet it's love that grants this, my high mission
Filled with noble ambition.
Her worth, when it takes my thought,
Shapes an image after my own wanting
That upon my sight plays, haunting,
Piercing deep within the heart
With clear power beyond the sun's full measure.
What should bring more pleasure
Than to be subdued through beauty's treasure
To her that Love has brought?

Through my sight, to the heart's deep core, she shot me
As a spark flies that's caught me
Blazing in Love's burning might
That can steal the full five senses of me
With a pure and lovely
Passion, so she cheats me of Love's right.
When against the weight of an ideal Love,
She sets you with your real Love
In the scales, though your heart takes joy to feel Love,
True Love weighs down Love's delight.

KEITH WALDROP

• • •

from: *THE CHANCES OF MAGIC*

u

Triple
city, built
by the damned.
Built from the earth,

the air, and the
space above our
air. City
allowed

a millenium of
ruin. Mercy
of mere
existence. After which,

by its — our — own
will, collapsing
like a dying
star into

a bull's-eye for a
single arrow.
All
over.

C. K. WILLIAMS

• • •

from: *THE LARK. THE THRUSH. THE STARLING*
[Poems from Issa]

That the world
is going
to end someday
does not concern
the wren:

it's time to
build your nest,
you build
your nest.

Spring: another
joke.

This run-down
house: me.

Go ahead, ask,
how's
spring?

Average, just
average.

RAE ARMANTROUT

•   ••

SINGLE MOST

Leaves fritter.

Teased edges.

It's vacillation that pleases.

Who answers for
the 'whole being?'

This is
only the firing

—

Daffy runs across
the synapses, hooting
in mock terror.

Then he's shown
on an embankment, watching
the noisy impulse pass.

—

But there's always a steady hum
shaped like a room
whose door must lead to
what really

where 'really'
is a nervous
tic as regular

—

as as   as as

the corner repeats itself

—

Dull frond:
giant lizard tongue
stuck out
in the murky distance
sight slides off
as a tiny elf.

—

Patients are asked to picture
health as an unobstructed
hall or tube
through which Goofy now tumbles:
Dumb luck!

Unimagined
creature scans postcard.

—

Conclusions can be drawn.

Shadows add depth
by falling

while deep secrets
are superseded—

quaint.

Exhaling
on second thought

MICHAEL DAVIDSON

THE LANDING OF ROCHAMBEAU

The Captain calls his crew to the deck
we are landing, he says
he doesn't know what to say next
so he adds, be back by noon me hearties
they don't believe him
this is not *Kidnapped*
and he would never use the word "hearties"
besides it is 1780, the harbor
is filled with sails
and the postmark covers some of them.

The Captain has gone below to pack
I have never landed before, he thinks,
what do I wear?
so he stands looking into the mirror
am I Rochambeau
or is this the name of my ship
or have we arrived at last in the Port
of Rochambeau where we will strike a deal
with natives, then he remembers
it is 1780, the water is jade green.

The Captain is astonished to learn
that the Colonies have defeated the British
because of a "Stamp Tax," we have landed
too late, he mourns and looks out the window
to his right (our left), tall masts jut
into the Fragonard sky
against which USA 10¢ is branded forever,
he approves of the lettering and decides
not to go ashore after all
but writes a postcard home:

We have landed, the Captain writes
but not very well: it is 1780 and they are rowing
out to meet us: it is impossible to tell
whether we are rowing or they are rowing
or who they might be; many sails fill
the harbor and the postmark is rolling towards us
from Brooklyn on the left (my right),
please advise: this is history and I am
caught in it without a thing to wear
if only my name were Napoleon.

As it is, my life takes up
only seven lines in *The Reader's Encyclopedia*
where it is clear that Washington and I
defeated Cornwallis at Yorktown
and with the French Fleet (which must explain
those sails!) forced "his" capitulation,
the entry leaves "his" a bit vague
in order to make the landing of Rochambeau
a surprise for both sides
including the reader's
who notices the pink sky of Watteau.

I am the Captain of this letter which begins
Dear Home, how I miss the Lisbon Earthquake
the Jansenist purges and leeks with egg,
remember Rochambeau in a foreign port
who must be content with corn and the inflated rhetoric
in pamphlets; I look up, he looks up
we regard him pausing mid-history
for a figure of speech like the ones he used to use
when writing Mme R. in Potsdam
like you are the author of my heart.

But it is 1780 and the Captain never writes postcards,
after all, he is a man of action
and he knows his fleet, the harbor
in which his ships lie at anchor,
he knows the sky, so common to USA
and the water, emerald blue
I'll go ashore, he says, throwing down his pen
and have a drink avec mon equipage
dans les petites boites du port
I know at last what to wear.

For I am Jean Baptiste Donatien de Vimeur
le Comte de Rochambeau and I have landed,
the water is blood red with history
and we are in its claws (he likes
the figure and writes it in his journal
then strides up to the deck
where the weather is clear)
"Lower the boats" he cries to a sailor,
"I will go ashore to The Bronx
where my name will be streets and parks."

But there is no sailor to hear him,
the deck is empty and the postmark
covers most of the fleet,
it has turned cold since Rochambeau landed
and when the French learn of what USA 10¢ means
they will cut off his title, Le Comte
no longer, only a name
in a time on a stamp on a card
for a reader who turns away from 1780
and remembers the water, white as their eyes.

JOHN HAWKES

•   •   •

from: *INNOCENCE IN EXTREMIS*

The days that followed came to the visitors like song birds to bits of varicolored glass in the sun. The crisp fall weather held. Their accommodations in the Old Gentleman's chateau followed exactly the discreet and orderly arrangements of their shipboard cabins, as if the Old Gentleman had somehow known in advance his ninth son's domestic dilemmas and had quite carefully placed the parents here, the sons there, the secretary here and the maids down there with the other domestics, thus assuring privacy and decency to all. There were feasts, there were toasts, one night they sat down to twenty geese, the next to whole coveys of pheasants in hunter's sauce, the next to a flock of roasted lambs. The pâtés, the sherbets, the dishes of glazed fruits outdid by far the dishes that the two French maids occasionally prepared to the cook's disapproval at Deauville Farms. The visitors were shown the countryside and entertained by chamber ensembles and by male singers whose basso voices might have belonged to Deauville heirs, and by female singers whose soprano voices were so pure and pleasing that they quite disguised their unmistakably erotic cast and gave virgin wings to their songs of insinuation and desire. The Irish matriarch and her mother-in-law did not know why they found the songs of the women singers so attractive, but so they did.

In the late mornings they all rode off to the hounds, except for the Irish matriarch and her mother-in-law, who followed the hunts in a light two-wheeled carriage. In the afternoons they strolled through the gardens, visited the chateaux of the Old Gentleman's nearest acquaintances. Darkness brought candlelight and celebrative meals and the inciting songs. Billy Boy was as good as gold; the Old Gentleman was kinder to Granny and tolerated Doc, and never again did he show to Uncle Jake his visage of inexplicable blame. Uncle Jake felt happier than he had ever been at Deauville Farms.

But the days of harmony and pleasure were further enhanced by certain occasions deemed by the Old Gentleman to be specially enjoyable to his assembly of delighted guests. The first took place before even a week had elapsed since their arrival.

One afternoon the bell in the Old Gentleman's private chapel began brightly ringing as for a wedding, and in the best of humors the Old Gentleman summoned everyone once more to the courtyard; with arms flung wide he herded them outdoors where they found awaiting them four rows of Empire chairs. The gilded frames and red plush cushions of the chairs shone in the agreeable light and contrasting as they did with the expanse of smooth and faintly purple, faintly pink cobblestones, moved everyone to exclamations of surprise and keen anticipation. The boys and their mother were seated in the front row.

Then the Old Gentleman gave a flourish with his right hand, curving the open and graceful old hand as might an impresario summoning an actor from his place of concealment in the wings. And in response to his flourish there came a tiny, sprightly clattering of hooves and through the gateway rode a young girl on a small and shapely dappled gray horse. Here was a sight to win them all and audibly they sighed and visibly they leaned forward. The girl, who was the youngest child of the Old Gentleman's eighth son, was the same age as Granny — fourteen — and though she had been shyly present in the chateau since this Deauville family reunion had commenced, she had from time to time caught Uncle Jake's attention when he had seen her firm young face in the candlelight, like a pale petal on a white china dish, or had spied her slipping gracefully into seclusion behind a mass of garrulous adults, still he had not been prepared for the vision she now presented to her already grateful audience. She looked like neither boy nor girl or like the best of both. She wore a trim black riding coat, a white stock, black boots and a black skirt that reached to her ankles. Best of all she wore a black silk hat which, befittingly small to suit her little head, nonetheless called to mind the larger and bolder silk hats generally worn by aristocratic men. Her dark brown hair was drawn tightly to her head and arranged in a short plait that barely touched the velvet collar of her coat. Around her silk hat, which was tilted becomingly forward, was tied a white silk ribbon that fluttered down the back of her neck and provided exactly the right touch of freedom and formlessness against the plait of hair. She was wearing gray gloves and riding side-saddle.

As for her horse, its size could not have been more appropriate to the size of its rider or its color and markings more complementary to her costume. The distance between the top of the girl's silk hat and the saddle, which was hidden beneath the skirts of the riding coat, was the same as from the saddle to the brightly varnished black hooves that were the size of teacups; when the breeze tossed up the gray silken tail in a filmy plume of abandon, the spread tail was a perfect counterpart to the horse's head and neck and rose to the height of the little creature's comely head. The gray mane was so long that it echoed the tail; the black colorations of the horse's legs were like tight stockings that mirrored the prim costume of the rider. The small gray horse looked like a hobbyhorse, its rider like a little man. Yet the horse was filled with the supplest life and no young girl could have sat upon its back more decorously than did the daughter of the Old Gentleman's eighth son. Together they were toy-like and so pretty that even the Old Gentleman in that moment watched his granddaughter with admiration and not the slightest sign of desire.

But the Old Gentleman had orchestrated the young girl's exhibition, for so it was to be, in such a way as to bring to absolute fruition the beauty of the young girl and her steed. He had gone so far as to choose the hour so that when the young girl stopped her horse in the center of the courtyard, as now she did, the sun was at such a distance above the westerly wall as to make fall across the cobblestones the largest and longest possible shadow of horse and rider. He had had the rows of chairs arranged at the eastern end of the courtyard so that his audience faced not only the girl and horse but, more important, the shadow that made them one and the same. He had even instructed his equestrienne to keep the head of her mount facing to the north throughout the performance so that she presented to her audience only her right side and never the left, and by so doing — since both her legs were positioned on the left side of the horse — created for her audience the illusion of a legless rider seated in perfect balance upon her horse. The fact that she appeared to have no legs was to the entire ensemble as was the white ribbon affixed to her hat: the incongruity without which the congruous whole could not have achieved such perfection.

There sat Uncle Jake leaning forward in the front row with his hands on his knees and his mouth open; there before him were the performers, quite motionless but for the fluttering ribbon and the mane and tail stirring in the breeze. With shame he thought of himself and his shaggy and dumpy pony back at Deauville Farms; with helpless ardor he beheld in the girl and her gray horse a vision of poise such as he thought would never again be his to savor.

The exhibition began. The miniature portrait came to life. The young girl did not move so much as a finger, as far as Uncle Jake could see, but her steed responded to her invisible command: it cocked its right front leg and then the left. And again. The reins were gently curving from the young girl's lowered hands to the silver bit; she was applying no tension to the reins. Now the horse moved sideways three paces, no more and no less, in Uncle Jake's direction, and then returned to its starting place and stopped. Then it took three paces forward and returned. And then the small full-bodied animal began to dance, as did the elongated shadow, and drummed with all four of its pretty hooves on the cobblestones in a medley of pure obedience to the girl it bore. It danced, it drummed, it turned, but never so far as to destroy the illusion of its impossibly legless rider, and all the while the girl disguised as a little man did not move but remained ever and easily vertical and did not vary in any way her pretty posture as the horse continued to captivate hosts and visitors alike in its dance.

Nearly everyone in that audience rode horseback. Most of them were fox hunters. Their lives depended on horses, whether or not they hallooed while hurtling over high fences, and whether or not they loved their massive mounts as much as they did their own children. Some of them secretly feared past injuries and those to come; a few had little aptitude for riding. Yet for all of them their mares and geldings and fillies and stallions were a matter of course like stones in a brook or birds in the boughs. Most of the horses they bred and rode were large, rugged, unruly, brutish beasts of great stamina. The horses raced and hunted, pulled their carriages, carried them ambling through sylvan woods and took them cantering great distances. But little more. So here in the Old Gentleman's courtyard the spectacle of the young equestrienne and her gray horse schooled only in dressage appealed directly to what they knew and to their own relationships to the horse and stable yet gave them all a taste of equestrian refinement that stirred them to surprise and pleasure. They had never thought of horseman-ship as an art, but here indeed in the dancing horse they could see full well the refinement of an artist's mind.

As they waited, hoping the finals would never come, the Irish matriarch, who for days had regretted that her past refusal to ride with her husband now prevented her from joining the Old Gentleman in the hunting field and consigned her instead to the two-wheeled carriage driven by her mother-in-law and from which she could see little of the old and brave patrician, suddenly found herself constrained to whisper behind her hand to Uncle Jake.

"Jake," she whispered, "mark my words, dear boy. That child is dangerous."

He was stunned. He envied the girl, he likened her to their youngest maid, he loved her, he wanted to become her and take her splendid place on the gray horse, even though he had no use for horses. Surely the girl who might have been his sister could not in any way be sinister, as his mother had said. He was confident that there was nothing sinister about her.

But the Irish matriarch, who was proud of her self-control, did not know why she had been so suddenly stung to spite by a young horse-woman as clearly innocent as her own second son. So quickly she added in a gentler voice: "But she is a beautiful little rider, Jake. You might try to ride as well as she does. It would please your father."

In his relief he smiled, leaned briefly toward the once more reassuring bulk of his mother, and returned to concentrating on the girl and the bobbing and swaying horse.

Then came the finale.

All at once and above the dainty clatter of the hooves, they heard the loud and charming tinkling of a music box. Heads turned, a new and livelier surprise possessed the audience, the fact that they could not discover the source of the music, which was the essence of artificiality, added greatly to the effect. Thanks to its quick and pretty strains that were suggestive of the tips of quills picking silver strings as fine as hair, the horse's dance attained its childlike crescendo while the rider allowed herself the faintest smile. The tempo of the music began to slow, with no distortion of its tinkling notes, and with it slowed the dance of the gray horse. The slower the music, the slower the dance; and just as the even longer spaces between the notes caused each note to stand increasingly alone as if it were to be the only one struck on the scale of poignancy, so the modulation of the horse toward motionlessness brought to a head the lovely aching quality of its movements. Then the music ceased, leaving behind its song in the silence, and the horse and rider grew so still that they might have been waxen figures in an equestrian museum. And then, with a slowness that brought everyone to the edge of his seat, the gray horse bowed. Out went its front legs, down came the head and neck and chest, lower and lower in the greatest possible contrast to the vertical line of the young girl, until the audience could no longer bear the nearly human tribute paid to it by the little horse and broke out in sustained and mellifluous applause. At once the animal returned to its proper stance, the girl laughed, and the horse and rider backed out of the courtyard and disappeared through the gate.

As one the audience rose to its feet, still clapping. They exclaimed aloud to each other, while clapping, and smiles vied with smiles and no one had praise enough for the exhibition which had taught them all that artificiality not only enhances natural life but defines it. Footmen came with trays of sherry, and the sunlight deepened, the voicing of appreciation grew softer, more lyrical. The Irish matriarch looked about for the Old Gentleman while Uncle Jake stayed close to her side and thought of the girl in the long skirts and black silk hat.

Then the Old Gentleman appeared and as one the audience realized that though they had all seen him act the impresario and with his raised hand start the performance, still he had not taken one of the red plush chairs for himself, had not been a passive witness to his granddaughter's exhibition. He was smiling broadly; he was perspiring; clearly he expected thanks. In all this the truth was evident: that not only had he himself orchestrated the day, but that it was he who had taught the girl dressage, and he who had from a little balcony conducted her performance and determined her every move, and he who had turned the handle of the music box. Never had the old patrician looked younger or more pleased with himself.

Weeks later, in the final days of their visit, when the Irish matriarch had learned well her lesson about the Old Gentleman and had suffered once more the full brunt of disillusionment, she remembered this afternoon of the dancing horse and thought, with a return of her terrible grimness, that even a lecherous man can be seduced into a state of the purest innocence.

MARGARET JOHNSON

•   •   •

from: *A VISIT TO THE CITIES OF CHEESE*

He tried so hard and is defeated. In the safehouse he lifts just the edge of the blind to peer out into the deserted street. They cannot be seen but they are of course there. The pavement of the street is wet and shining under the streetlights. There is music from another room. The inevitable sea laps at the pier.

He has associated himself with failure. A historical figure. Are you using me as a credit reference. In his prison he can't feel anything. It's September 1952. These bad things are going to happen, no suspense. He is feeling his way blindly through the prison. Should it not be September. Should it not be this month of this year. Maybe not September. How do you follow this tortuous route and tell the truth? He was radiant on the morning of his death. I'm not unhappy and they are all dead a long time ago, mid-1952. They want so badly to kill the language that they even burn the books of the writers they like. I followed you into the bushes. What a lovely city you showed me there, and how industrious all the people were. An industry of forgetting. I was not placid, I was willing to let go of a number of things in order to see your face. Reborn, he thought, this time they will understand me. But there is such a pleasant safehouse set aside for you. A little garden, forsythia, splash of yellow and your mother's lilacs. We take a turn through the garden, arm in arm, I in the red coat I wore as a child, you in galoshes. How lovely, spring, wet April. This is the principle of change, that we lost a lot. He is so pleased to have finally been able to set down his ideas in order, and maybe, when the examining authorities read them, they will understand that he is harmless, and let him go.

JACKSON MAC LOW

"THE WAVES BROKE ON THE SHORE."

(Six poems drawn from
Virginia Woolf's *The Waves*, pp. 116-41,
by means of its last sentence, 12 August, 1976)

1.

then this the whom say Neville;
together.

Louis,
boot.

drum about rocket.

golden of entirely this that the
stability
Who
Who over ourselves to the
the which table wavering
unreal waits being.

cruelty should looks ancient of
instinct these the
When she which door.

there nailed to
"Rhoda
She waiter,
basin.

pavements makes opens,

2.

brings order.

flow forks blazed.

of on the
the
the so shabby door course opera
perception that that opera
waves salute;
love were turns
But are Rhoda.

sink forget our in their
The breath scatters the door
heart oppression
The chaos over.

when takes loves,
other's heels been cracked
closer darkness secrecy on and
this changing,
feeling scullery-maid the among
every bowler tightly through
even white had severance tapers,
pages boards,

3.

drawing from took dawned on
and throats,
shook
"The swallow the Rhoda.

There flower to which every
world talk."

lived lives thousands beast
Arab should seek pattern.

of under the
the opens stand the door,"
door perfection through the
the with fail love.

makes gives by grow Rhoda,
spike mailed or and the things
pretend,
Susan,
them spot,
peered carpets to through fields
watch hare?

love,

4.

hate,
dress be wrinkled crops back
waves of under than the
the seasons.

shall Rhoda,
where sullen,
the shall see wall hate love
ob-
ject shows by tree-tops.

knowing smoke alone of and
that Rhoda
She shatter the whoever
character
There the that used went caps
loved care,
slips beech trees,

whom talk,
perfect of into than there when
silent the "Look,"
everywhere;
range this through queer which
have have spread themselves
before."

5.

cries hoots.

forks,
walled outside."

India,"
the shore;
see stamped that among pair endless,
the
There are wears language five
Oriental rides blood.

trance look—
darkness;
scope,
of and trees,
the
the say,
this,
from fear.

differences.

the what there whirling hate,

6.

love,"
stream makes but from
"upon weak false of and
those that seem spread the
Rhoda whirlpool between
to Rhoda,
where wings dark moving,
knee makes beckon,
dreams.

from looking street."

of One then the then so
that Rhoda,
blares
There the
the
the which have living rise
horns blue are violets.

deck laurel on
And
The shadow are some the flows
swerve
There there the lie white,

RON SILLIMAN

•   •   •

from: *PARADISE*

When that april with his sure as soot the draft of March has pierced it to the root and bothered every vein in swish liqueur of which virtue engendered is the floor. Damp earth dusts the leaves of a new transplanted violet. Thousands in Denver flee big acid cloud. The bath mat, a deep red, needs shaking. The dresser lacks handles. Big sun wobbles up through branches of the plum tree. Objects repeated take on value. The ostrich is a pretty bird (false). A ceramic jar full of brown sugar. Old bristle brush kept beneath sink. I remover the article. The way an old sponge goes sour. In the valley cars move slowly, crowding into the city. In the papers orchestrated lies compete for space. In the prepositional the temporality of syntax mimes space. Rhyme violates reason: thus I remember.

The street crew hunkers low against the side of the building, passing a pack of cigarettes down the line without comment, safety vests a brilliant orange. A row of robins. Without speech, Eyes fixed upon a passerby. The smoke blue and quickly shape-less in the light breeze. In the gutter a dustbroom lies next to a mound: leaves, paper, glass. This never happened. The world represented is not that world. In one where the wind whips through the eucalyptus, Reagan is never President. The hand is seen jutting from the sleeve. Pain is not questioned. But the moment between sentences. The crowd roars as the rightfielder hurls a strike right to the plate. While from the sideview this is seen as sculpture, smooth, carved, timeless. The gallery's silence is not the garden's. Old trees have been cleared away. Now we use them as benches or as propositions. In that one Gerald Ford is an eternal ideal. Do hummingbirds envy? The organization of dust on a hillside more careful than Chartres. But the moment between sentences, words. Green tables. Are not absent. Count for something.

Plum tree fuller, more green. Two birds, twittering, trash around in it. In the shade, a chill breeze undercuts the clean blue slate of sky, sun barely above the rooftops. It's yellow, but whitens as it rises. In the blanket of baby-tears at the base of the tree, a snail stretches its full body, crossing toward the shed. I want to call those prongs antlers. The sun shines right through its yellow-green body.

Comp time. Little words inching into syntax, itching into context. The margin of morning. The white space is not silence. The mysterious flea market where all the Deadheads buy their clothes. They lurch out of the doorways with their palms up. Gradually the cereal absorbs the milk. Tiny green plums start to appear. Soon the fuchsia will start to blister. Dull white sun heavy in the sky. This guy calls me Spike. The rotted stairs wobble. A green hamper. Old pipes rise out of the roofs right over the kitchens. To touch them, books in this climate are cool and damp. Countertransference (the writer doesn't "like" the reader). Cords hang from sockets. The last player to make an unassisted triple play was Ron Hansen, a graduate of Albany High. That key on the latch by the back door is to the lock we never use.

The small children rise in the wind, drifting, long shoelaces tangled all the way back down to the treetops. One corner just to keep brooms in. Simple single syllable. The weight of the dog against the wood of the fence, snarling. The dull distant televised stare of a president.

Words do drift, black on whatever lighter background. Another impulse brightens the face into a silly grin. The script of the neon lettering is florid. No accounting for syllables here. The whole yard brightens into day long before the sun's up. The garbagemen have their own cans, which are larger and on wheels. The ink is an oily film on a metal ball that turns as the pen rolls over the paper. I am not in love with the punctuation. Government enforces new math of binding. In the dream the married woman pulls up her skirt.

All the dogs begin to howl. Pigeon's gray a camouflage for concrete. It's going to be a hot one. All these small, off-white, stucco homes. Sharp smell of ripe banana. The point beyond which poetry is a curse. The leaves of the noun grown too hard and spotted. Teenage girls in white painter's pants. Writing the bus. His face was no longer simple. Old sheets used as curtains, knotted on a sunny day.

New morning, sawdust on the unfinished porch. Follow the machine of the hand up the cables to the wrist. Visible cows. On a day this hot you can smell the sun. Coffee fills the kitchen.

The promise of an old Braxton heard like a chore, sore throat. The whole family, dressed to the nines, piles into the dark car. A week at work. White curtains along the kitchen windows, the high fogged sky behind them just as white.

In the wake of bells. Pose a minute, hand pulling softly at lobe of ear. Yellow dog seems to smile. In the market no one speaks your language. All of human history leading up to a stiff neck. The hanging ferns swing gently to mark the quake. She glances back at you over her shoulder. The plane's approach fills the screen until it rises, passing over. The mode of reading we call doggy-style. The neutrality of the headline is brazen, unreal. What architect planned that shed?

BARBARA EINZIG

•• •

READING FOR PLEASURE

He wrote that the light struck the window blind and he should have stopped there, as he had stopped to see it, struck, the light, the glass. These things are repeated forever and we attempt to read and understand them, the way one reads a poem, and one stops in the reading over and over while going on.

Searching behind the pronoun in the dark looking with the hands for a false wall. This is who I am. Don't take it personally. How can I help it. This kind of poetry she criticizes as a form of packaging, but we want to open our eyes.

The ocean he said is humiliating in its disguises. Encantados are pure spirit, they have no shadows. A sentence certainly looks forward and backward and that makes a darkness around its line, nimbus. These are buildings that make things happen inside or outside, and all people open windows as far as I know.

They brought up the child in the usual way, but without a name. Others struggled to name him in order to call him, but to no avail, they only let out a sound which struck the back of his steadily larger head, the way it would hit a lamp post. When he got to an age when he was open to discussing personal matters with some trace of objectivity, he was firmly persuaded a name was a necessary aspect of being human, and at this time he took on the name Norman, though it never seemed to fit him.

The feathers of the birds are red or orange or blue or green, colors unknown to a bird or as words to viewers in a foreign climate. The words just pour out like water, splashing or being absorbed into the ground. Do you consider writing a form of self-expression, either in the formation of the letters themselves, as in calligraphy, or in what thoughts or meanderings these characters compose?

Slowly things get rich, as if underwater, forms multiply in the grace of color. Steel blue with black stripes, fish swim in water imaginary as the past. What is made up is the coral reef, with its symbiosis and clown fish hiding like words. In the turtle's eight-foot-long body, in its gigantic swimming, comparisons vanish and turn to silence.

Maybe something is orange here, something may be poisonous, the stone fish in its generous shape disappears. Red fish match the underside of coral.

I saw these small fish once before in dust swimming in sunlight slowly things were poor in air and moved without halting. I drew in the air and it was clean or dirty; I stood in the sun yellow and streaming or behind a cloud. I stand back and I look out the window; my face is hidden in the darkness you see.

People who view me as another species are living around me. Others come to me looking for the truth. Slowly culture disappears into the culture of a photograph, into a voice without location. On the ground my feet complain and suffer.

Danger is a relative matter terribly linked with knowledge. My eyesight isn't what it used to be. The sentences are each letters mailed from different countries, arriving to tell their stories after they have occurred.

Despite their impoverishment, nevertheless they bear witness. By repeating what they are saying over and over, though incomprehensible, the nature of what they have endured becomes clear.

Some have cut vast stones out of the faces of mountains; the hair of some turns red from malnutrition. These things are recorded fairly simply — in their own images, if with imperfect exposure. The things I say end with their own breath; they vanish and turn to silence; their repetitions now falter evenly as the steps of very old people do when they walk.

My age is the age I live in. My costume mimics another era.

The spell here is made out of its breaking, out of the startling rise of a school. I could have made you happier by telling you a story of someone who left for work and came home to dinner. But some of those who left for work have disappeared, but all of those who leave for work disappear. Made out of my own language, flayed, transported, forgiven. The messages I find in weather are eternal. Everyone in the village wears the same hat.

Imagine that, a city grown over, four generations of Incas living in an unknown spot. I see a face in the coral and you do also. The windows are without glass, wooden they open inward. You turn your memory into my voice and I turn my memory in yours, gigantic swimming of our relation. The air I drew in turns into an outward breath, word or song. They are surrounded by solids, fluids and gases. They are surrounded by things they cannot see that they understand through their minds, that they hold in mind.

Imagine that, a language grown over, once people lived there, once people lived inside those structures we see from above, on the wall as colored light.

PETER GURNIS

•   ••

from: *THE BODY OF LIBERTIES*

Metacomet
Wampanoag
Narragansett
and the Pequot
delivered into our hands

and the beast
shall be slain
and buried
and not eaten

and after the earthquake a fire
as a cloud to a window

but why at this Cape?

the day was pointed with hail
with nothing to eat
but a pint of barnacles

the most crooked way that was ever gone

who can stay his hand
with pungent discourse?

ELIZABETH ROBINSON

•   • •

THE NEW LANGUAGE

for George

I

Given the limitation of trees, what if each
season of leaves produces a bowl?

The machine of language has soft flesh;
a dirt portal has no room for roots but intends

that you speak gently.

And this bowl has hands of its own.

The hands claim that each flavor requires a name
and then that fragrance can manifest itself in juice and rind.

Any grove can promise this lexicon.

II

And given the discourse of seasons,
mouths are irrelevant.

The machine leaps up on the basis of what's foreign.

The fruit tends to forgive words;
it's an estrangement that turns
to mulch.

It's the shape of a body in a grove, everything sudden.

III

Inside the mouth, it's winter.
And no other cistern will convey

how a system has to release its own grammar
and fruit falls everywhere and a body should have to be
deft

and without trespass,

another form of the bowl rounding.

IV

The stem, the branch, the arc of the arm.
Say something now, under the awkwardness of law.

And dirt and skin combine.
It is impossible to see what was said before.
And blossoms issue from the tongue, but no memory.
And the newness of the phrase is obscured by its orchard.
And the stem is too tender.

Better than fecundity are lists.

V

What could marry the density of a seed to the explicit word
but hardness?

This clothes a bare arm while leaves fall and fall.

ROBERT CREELEY

•• •

THE COMPANY

Backward — as if retentive.
"The child is father to the man"
or some such echo of device,
a parallel of use and circumstance.

Scale become implication.
Place, postcard determinant —
only because someone sent it.
Relations — best if convenient.

"Out of all this emptiness
something must come..." Concomitant
with the insistent banality, small, still
face in mirror looks simply vacant.

Hence blather, disjunct, incessant
indecision, moving along on
road to next town where what waited
was great expectations again, empty plate.

So there they were, expectably ambivalent,
given the Second World War
"to one who has been long in city pent,"
trying to make sense of it.

We — *morituri* — blasted from classic,
humanistic *noblesse oblige*, all the garbage
of either so-called side, hung on
to what we thought we had, an existential

raison d'être like a pea
some faded princess tries to sleep on,
and when that was expectably soon gone,
we left. We walked away.

Recorders ages hence will look for us
not only in books, one hopes, nor only under rocks
but in some common places of feeling,
small enough — but isn't the human

just that echoing, resonant edge
of what it knows it knows,
takes heart in remembering
only the good times, yet

can't forget whatever it was,
comes here again, fearing this
is the last day, this is the last,
the last, the last.

SONG

What's in the body you've forgotten
and that you've left alone
and that you don't want —

or what's in the body that you want
and would die for —
and think it's all of it —

if life's a form to be forgotten
once you've gone and no regrets,
no one left in what you were —

That empty place is all there is,
and/if the face's remembered,
or dog barks, cat's to be fed.

LAURA CHESTER

•   •   •

from: *FREE REIN*

The search to get lost in a great big coat. "I dreamt that indigo was the drug of the gentry. Certain tastes I've always had." Take up courage and walk into the kitchen. This worked, by her upright name. Throw prerequisites all to the wind (in which we're whirling). *Stick with me kid.* Make it burn. He dreamt she was in love with another mood, darker. She dreamt of antlers that stretched across the room. Fresh white birch that looks like chicken meat. Cold breast tastes like chicken-of-the-woods. The mind snaps backward like a piece of elastic, to the image, words, repeat performance. "I dreamt of kissing Kenny who had this respect for me." We'll know when we get there because we'll all have mouths. That's no preacher, that's a creature! Emptying your pockets full of burden in the river. You don't know what it's like, to be living alone.

Until one night, over the banquet she remembered, the original Eagle, and as she spoke, his eyes were lit with a lovely alertness. "But why this horse," her Grandmother asked her. All the way from Montana. "Because I love him," she said, and her breath made a whiteness. She could hardly believe that her heart had been heard. Together they went to the stockyard. All the dirt lanes were empty and floodlit, as they wandered the maze, calling his name, until she saw the fire of his form — Greeted by an anxious, displaced whinny, mountain pony — She climbed the ten foot rails into the pen. No one else could control him. That fast. No one else dared to ride him. "My horse." But finally, at thirty-six, when they led him down the dump road, all the other horses came to the field edge and whinnied. He was gone before the needle was empty. Can you buy another Eagle for a dollar? Can you climb back into the fire of the pen? Can you even dare to say, "But I love him," again, and try to make everything possible.

LISSA McLAUGHLIN

• • •

MRS. SHREEVE AND MRS. BOLERO

1. Mrs. Shreeve on the Ledge

If you look over you will see two things. A thin forearm so much like a stick it strikes you as shocking, reaching around in thin air through the absent bottom of a large two-pane window — the hand reaching up over the enormous pane above with a sponge in continuous circles — and beneath the glass, which shimmers like a skin, the blurred bent hump of the rest of Mrs. Shreeve, standing directly behind the glass, her little reddened mouth open in a way she wouldn't want you to see. She's panting in a hard, pained way. Like she's going inside out. But she hides this fastidiously, more veins horning up to the surface of her face every day, while her skin moves slowly sideways. Just like your grandmother who sat in armchairs lifting forearms over the teacups and dessert plates in shrewd minced ways trying not to look hungry while she shoved her beautiful ankles back under the chair because they were shiny suddenly, full of fluid. A condition of the heart, years ago she pulled her ankles free from farm shit under her armpits swore all that off and now the sounds of cows blowing out hard from her own coughing mouth. A sound Mrs. Shreeve makes now suddenly against the window. You hear it, next door you spend a long time near that window. You push your pencils back and forth. For a minute you're scared she's going to crawl out. Then you tell yourself, That's Mrs. Shreeve. Nothing can happen. The bright sponge pokes unceremoniously through air. And a look of scorn is on her tiny face attacking the glass, you see her mouth go up and down, her blurred coughing move back and forth, she rattles the glass. Don't do it.

2. *Grandmas Make Great Lovers*

Mrs. Shreeve is hot to go in the car with Mrs. Bolero. Grandmas Make Great Lovers says the bumper-sticker. Mrs. Shreeve picked it out for Mrs. Bolero. Now we have to drive like that, said Mrs. Shreeve. They approach an intersection. To their left the other driver lifts his head under his hat, waves them through, gazing at him they rise simultaneously on the seat as if to call Thank you! When they're safely by Mrs. Bolero grips the wheel and asks, Who was that man? Mrs. Shreeve only has time to twist in her seat. Adjusting its blinkers left and right the car makes its progress and the ladies' hands also point. The car is approaching another intersection and if you peek at Mrs. Shreeve her face is still headed backward at the man, reduced and laconic, densely tied by wrinkles.

3. *Specialties of the House*

Specialties of the house include: spaghetti and sausages or spaghetti and meatballs, fried eggplant, Greek spinach pie, cube steak. This last they have to break into shape with a mallet. A guy out back dribbles egg yolk over the spinach pie. This unforeseen violence hangs in the air even as the ladies push open the front door. Hello? they yell, Anyone here? After a minute they stop looking at each other and see a guy coming to seat them. He's Louie, one of the cooks, two menus in his hands and his arms frothing with black hair. Hi, Louie, the ladies say. Having a nice day, Louie? asks Mrs. Shreeve into Louie's white sleeve as he shifts their chairs for them. Yeah, I guess, says Louie and walks away. When he's gone Mrs. Shreeve bends forward, I see five flies. Does it make you suspicious? Well, just pretend you don't, answers Mrs. Bolero. She studies her menu calmly while Mrs. Shreeve hits at the flies. Mrs. Bolero always orders one of two things. Actually, this is one place she's decided is completely safe. Closing her menu she examines the blossom in the vase in front of her. With one finger she pushes it toward Mrs. Shreeve. With her grave broad face of a saint Mrs. Bolero enjoys an acute sense of what to say. Here, she says, Smell.

4. They Sit in the Back Yard

They sit in the back yard. You can see them though you're running back and forth with half your clothes on, trying to get ready for work. Why are you so attracted? You, who have a job and can look at almost anything? Because you resent them, their forthrightness, the forthrightness of dogs or cats foraging nakedly in the street, or of one hair showing on a scalp. You can imagine Mrs. Bolero exclaiming to Mrs. Shreeve with sudden fright, Why Blanche, your face attracts me like a single hair lying on a counter! Sometimes your own disappointments rise up along the window like steam, and you want to see these two begin to argue, attacking each other as the bitter fruit of one another's sinking bodies. You want to hear them start shouting, You have nothing to do with me, get out of here! You want to see them start chasing each other around, screaming at each other like hyenas. You'd like to see them refuse to admit to the existence of any squirrels up in the tree. Instead they spot squirrels easily and can watch them for hours. Today a dead squirrel lies in the grass. Mrs. Bolero gets up and goes over to it. A cat got it, she says. They get up, two old women opened and soft as rags, and peer closely and with gentle concentration into the stab wounds of the squirrel.

5. Mrs. Bolero's Hair

Mrs. Bolero's hair has the knotty translucence of fishline. The ends fork like lightning. She combs it hard, too hard for her hairdresser. What are you doing? You're pulling it all out! The hairdresser is at her wits' end with Mrs. Bolero. Mrs. Bolero's mother was very small and intense, Portuguese. The doctor told Mrs. Bolero one day she'd better stop washing herself so much, she was taking away too much skin. Quit this every day business, he said, One bath every three days even may be too often. Mrs. Bolero's skin hurt her so much she couldn't forget what he said. She was ashamed and afraid of herself for several months after this. She kept sniffing. OK Doctor, she said. Years after, smelling soap, she still feels, under the doctor's dimming voice, her mother's heavy head, shaking.

6. Mrs. Shreeve Under the Weather

Mrs. Shreeve fell ill. Mrs. Bolero came to see her. She described the action of the traffic in the street. She mentioned dogs she had seen. The doctor prescribed a regimen of steam. Both women thanked him. Mrs. Bolero ran the vaporizer. High sighs came from Mrs. Shreeve's chest. The ladies looked at each other. Mrs. Bolero went over and watched some dirt cling fiercely to the outside of the window. Mrs. Shreeve felt a little better. The doctor said she was perfect. Mrs. Shreeve looked at him. She had noticed the dirt on the window.

7. Two Ladies

Two ladies do without husbands over the long term. Two ladies develop pet names for each other. Two ladies call out in the night. Two ladies like treats. Two ladies penetrate distant and more local stores for sales. Two ladies fail to scorn illness. Two ladies avoid one another's doctors. Two ladies watch one conspicuous vein after another rise to the surface. Two ladies divulge numerous intimate secrets under the guise of discussing the calamities that can befall any physical woman. Two ladies search for certain articles of apparel no longer popular. Two ladies experience palpitations before it is morning. Two ladies recall outmoded swear words. Two ladies develop rodent habits of storage and tension. Two ladies feel diminished. Two ladies realize quiet misrepresents panic. Two ladies sweat. Two ladies feel quickly across surfaces for the pressure of new appearances. Two ladies open letters. Two ladies touch nightgowns to their uplifted feet. Two ladies dust, knocking over chairs. Two ladies sweep furiously. Two ladies still listen to their mothers, their soft injunctions. Two ladies look up from waiting. Two ladies still recognize a doorknob. Go to the window. Lean out, like a squirrel motioning the light sideways with its hand.

CRAIG WATSON

•   •º

CURRENCY

for V. B.

change hands.
what fits.

    the screen door at which breeze glimpses and stutters.

    the membraneous night.

    the still, the single, the instead of.

    the sculpted open empty mouth

---

try to maintain a profile

a figure chalked by eclipse
    facsimile
    surrogate
guest of the present

        at rest, resisted

and give to you
for receipt:

the coin equals its activity,
passing from palm to palm.

then what happens
must happen.

offered or taken, as if
for one you do the other

even when two-for-one
until out, in debt

surrendered to and swallowed by
mirrors

clenched in the blades
of their gaze

---

cancel skin.

defeat choice.

cling to names-of-things wrung from particular silences.

because a lie is the responsibility of the listener

and in its cracked shell ear hears only own breath
hiss and ring, anonymous

the eye moves
the wall snaps.

lie still.
as if here and

multiplied by one.

in the next moment,
the last moment.

the assault by
every object.

the wake of
sudden sameness.

---

slabs of curved air
acres of wall
disappearing distances
glasses of water

neither a point of impact
nor not *not* here.

so interrupted, dismembered

so divided, devoured

so invisible, impossible

there is no catharsis.

beauty is an order which
devours its monuments,
maintaining something (someone)
to let go of

    resuming indifference

_____

then the piece-work light
its descent to own skin in
blank sheets and thin shadows

or a smothering mist
sponged from iridescent dough
of a common sky

turn away
turn around
turn away

TINA DARRAGH

•• •

from: *PIE IN THE SKY*

) *PART 2* (
Long Arms — sounds as clichés

"Stretch out your arm & I'll stretch out
mine. Let's measure them. No one has
as long an arm as I have. SEE! I have
really long arms!"

Long Arms

moola

"mool" started as a variation of "gool" (gold) indicating farmland
freshly plowed and ready to be worked. This aspect of "ready"
leads to a second meaning — dry bread broken into a bowl as a sop
for the liquid there. Mingling of solid and liquid lead to a third
definition — to associate intimately. Adding "a" to "mool"
switches us over to religion where it is a corruption of "mullah"
— a Moslem learned in theology.

razz-ma-tazz

"razz" was first "razzia", an Algerian expression for a
quick-as-a-flash military raid. When later added to "dazzle" as
a description of a football play, it took on the properties of
electricity, as in "I'm going to razzle-dazzle the boys with my
great lightning change act" or "There isn't enough real down-
right razzle-dazzle here to run a milk cart." During vaudeville,
the dazzle was altered to "tazz" to accent the "z" in "razz", the
same buzz made by the footlights used to brighten the stage.

sis boom ba

sis	co wet
	era
	kin
	ley
	mondi
	iten
	y
	ter
	tine
	troid
	trum
	yphus

boom

The first "boom" heard was the coastline cry of the bittern. A similar "boom" is that made by waves hitting wood, as in the floating timber used to partition part of a harbor or the spar run out to extend the foot of a sail or the pole used to push a boat off from land.

ba

A lower case "b" used with a "," can stand for bar, barn or black. A capital "B" used with a "." and a "," stands for bass or basso or bay or Bible or bolivar or boliviano or book or born or breadth or British or brother. A lower case "b" with a "." stands for baseball or bay or "blend of" or born. Capital "B" with a dash stands for Boeing. Lower case "b" with a lower case "a" can mean human-headed bird or the second letter of the Arabic alphabet. A capital "B" with a lower case "a" denotes "barium." A capital "B" with a "." and a capital "A" with a "." can mean Bachelor of Arts, bastard amber or British America. Another "a" added to "ba" gives us "bleat" and a double "ba" leaves us with a molded rum raisin cake literally taken from the expression "old woman."

HARRY MATHEWS

•
 •
 •

from: *OUT OF BOUNDS*

Absent so often, you leave open a rough way back — to enjoy, to decide
The knowledge which sometimes is better viewed in the first jelled pecking
    trough of memory,
Safe from the doomed jackal that waits to pounce on the bevy
Of presences yet more blackly doomed: true, we injure when we shrive them,
Ourselves less than probable judges (because they feed on us as we also
    on them);
Still, not hoping for my salvation, I hold unjoking to your way, inscribing
    my fatal words to "you".

————

The blink of abrupt joy conceals beneath the swerving of my forehead
Two twinkling springs it sometimes in vehement dejection confusedly bursts.
Now, however, the fervent, needy heart breaks them open in a sorrowful
    ejaculation that cannot lie
(An ejaculation incapable of self-cure by venial remedies like: keeping
    patience with her perfection)
From lack of power to endure what moves the heart to joy and beggary:
A withdrawal, a removal, a taking-back, a jovial parting of that holy
    goal of my infatuation.

————

So, at the hour of death, when I pass, sink, or crash into that vacancy
    beyond injury or delight,
Enveloped in the dusky cerements of another most loved, most winning
    friend, beyond even juvenile
Abandon, when her jewelled arms stretch lustrously white (a familiar
    pallor in the sea-rocked dark)
And her eyes, whose flicker reveals no brilliance but their own, reflect
    neither space nor time, rather conjure their opposites:
Your eyes can then acknowledge these words and find joy among the
    evoked beauties of your youth,
And in that shining you will justify this our last collusion, and from it I
    shall pluck my only survival.

91

••   •

from: *TWELVE PARTS OF HER*

if the voice spoke Venetian blind

                                    •   her
                                                     mouth
                                                     a
                                                     wall
                                                     of
                                                     talk
                                                     resents
                                                     a
                                                     position
                                                     in
                                                     which
                                                     his
                                                     mouth
                                                     takes
                                                     part
                                                     being
                                                     part
                                                     mold

                                                     part
                                                     figure

                                                     twelve
                                                     parts
                                                     marble

9   such a series refuses the laundry and walks with a
    haughty stride which succeeds in creating a sound of
    disquiet. . .

then the arches surrender to marble

●

not
of
her
at
all

10 "if not the case then what is!" "perhaps we should make that call?" "don't think this has anything to do with the final decision!" "perhaps you would like a drink with a twist? . . ."

WALTER ABISH

•   ••

WHAT ELSE (Part II)

> In using selected segments of published texts authored by others as the
> exclusive "ready made" material for these five "explorations," I want-
> ed to probe certain familiar emotional configurations afresh, and arrive
> at an emotional content that is not mine by design.... The European
> pseudo-autobiography, "What Else," was obtained from 50 self-por-
> traits, journals, diaries, and collected letters.

198

I was on an English boat going from Siracusa in Sicily to Tunis in North
Africa. I had taken the cheapest passage and it was a voyage of two
nights and one day. We were no sooner out of the harbor that I found in
my class no food was served. I sent a note to the captain saying I'd like to
change to another class. He sent a note back saying that I could not
change and, further, asking whether I had been vaccinated. I wrote
back that I had not been vaccinated and that I didn't intend to be. He
wrote back that unless I was vaccinated I would not be permitted to
disembark at Tunis. We had meanwhile gotten in a terrific storm. The
waves were higher than the boat. It was impossible to walk on the
deck. The correspondence between the captain and myself continued in
a deadlock. In my last note to him, I stated my firm intention to get off his
boat at the earliest opportunity and without being vaccinated. He then
wrote back that I had been vaccinated and to prove it he sent along a
certificate with his signature.

66

The writer of this book is no misanthrope; today one pays too dearly for
hatred of man. If one would hate man the way man was hated formerly,
Timonically, wholly, without exception, with a full heart, and with the
whole love of hatred, then one would have to renounce contempt. And
how much fine joy, how much graciousness ever do we owe precisely to
our contempt!

121

I play my role. Only in the plane or hotel into which promoters have booked me am I for a while alone and under no obligation to maintain anything. I take a bath or a shower, then stand at the window—a view of another city. A twinge of stage fright, every time. While reading, I forget each word the moment I have read it. Afterward a cold buffet. To the same questions I do not always return the same answers, for I do not find any of my answers all that convincing. I watch a lady's nice teeth from close up as she speaks to me; I hold a glass in my hand, and I sweat. This is not my metier, I think to myself, but here I stand.

85

Sometimes the weary traveler suffering from jetlag prefers to be shown directly to his hotel to be sewn in the sheets from which no dreams ever befalls. Weary and heartsick, emotionally battered by the voyage, the eyes overcome with fatigue, unable to read the newspaper thoughtfully provided for him he teeters on the hem of sleep, disrobing this way or that, clenching in his teeth all these distraught objects of the recent past — the way someone looked at him, seeming not seeing but just seeing.

83

Since I have been famous, neckties, caps, handkerchiefs, and whole sentences complete with instruction for use have been stolen from me. (Fame is someone it seems to be fun to piss on.) The more famous a man gets the fewer friends he has. It can't be helped: fame isolates. When fame helps you he never lets you forget it. When he hurts you, he says something about the price you have to pay. I certify that fame is boring and only rarely amusing.

195

Sousse, Sfax, the great Ranan circus at El Djem, Kairouan, Djerba — I reach them all without difficulty by train, by bus and by boat. At Djerba, Ulysses had forgotten Penelope and Ithaca: the island was worthy of its legend. It was a cool orchard with a carpet of dappled grass; the glossy crowns of palms sheltered by the delicate blossoming trees; the edges of this garden were lashed by the sea. I was the only guest at the hotel and the owner spoiled me. She told me that the summer before, one of her boarders, a little English girl, had gone every day to a deserted beach to lie in the sun; one day she came back to lunch, her face all crumpled, and did not touch her food. "What's the matter?" my hostess asked; the girl burst into tears. Three Arabs who had been watching her for several days, had raped her, one by one. "I tried to cheer her up," the woman said. "I said to her: Oh! Mademoiselle, when you are travelling. . . Come now, calm yourself; after all, when you are travelling!" But she insisted on packing her bags that same evening.

92
A disturbed night in spite of the pill. Dreamt angrily of someone of whom I have never waking thought angrily.

Conrad's *Heart of Darkness* still a fine story, but its faults show now. The language too inflated for the situation. Kurtz never really comes alive. It is as if Conrad had taken an episode in his own life and tried to lend it, for the sake of "literature," a greater significance than it will hold. And how often he compares something concrete with something abstract. Is this a trick I have caught.

45
June 22.
Now the itch to write is over, the vacuum in my brain begins again. My novel is finished, I feel a twinge of rheumatism or arthritis. Is it that you can feel only one thing at a time, or do you imagine them?

154
The day before yesterday we were in the house of a woman who had two others there for us to lay. The place was delapidated and open to all the winds and lit by the night-light, we could see a palm tree through the unglassed window, and two Turkish women wore silk robes embroidered with gold. This is a great place for contrasts: splendid things gleaming in the dust. I performed on a mat that a family of cats had to be shooed off—a strange coitus, looking at each other without being able to exchange a word, and the exchange of looks is all the deeper for the curiosity and surprise. My brain was too stimulated for me to enjoy it otherwise. These shaved cunts make a strange effect—the flesh is as hard as bronze, and my girl has a splendid arse.

Goodbye—Write to me, write to my mother sometimes...

148
Oct. 14.
I get up early and go to the dining room for coffee. Everybody bows and I bow and I can't remember any of their names or what they are doing

here. I know some of them are journalists, some of them are working for the government, and most of them are foreigners, but they swim as one except for a tall, pale young Frenchman and a German couple who shake hands with affection as they part each morning in front of the hotel. I have done nothing since I am here and I recognize the signs. I have presented my credentials, as one must, gone once to the Press Office where I was pleasantly welcomed by Constancia de la Mora, had two telephone calls from her suggesting I come back to the office and meet people who might like to meet me, and have not gone.

143

Jackdaws inhabit the village. Two horses are feeding on the bark of a tree. Apples lie rotting in the wet clay soil around the trees, nobody is harvesting them. On one of the trees, which seemed from afar like the only tree left with any leaves, apples hung in mysterious clusters close to one another. There isn't a single leaf on the wet tree, just wet apples refusing to fall. I picked one, it tasted pretty sour, but the juice in it quenched my thirst. I threw the apple core against the tree, and the apples fell like rain. When the apples had becalmed again, restful on the ground, I thought to myself that no one could imagine such human loneliness. It is the loneliest day, the most isolated of all. So I went and shook the tree until it was utterly bare.

111

Back from Morocco, I once sat down with eyes closed and legs crossed in a corner of my room and tried to say "Allah! Allah! Allah!" over and over again for half-an-hour at the right speed and volume. I tried to imagine myself going on saying it for a whole day and a large part of the night; taking a short sleep and then beginning again; doing the same thing for days and weeks, months and years; growing older and older and living like that, and clinging tenaciously to that life; flying into a fury if something disturbed me in that life; wanting nothing else, sticking to it utterly.

97

There is something else too. When Doughty went to Arabia in the 1800s, he claimed somewhat grandly that it was to revive the expressive possibilities of the English language. Well, in a sense, I also went to the desert to solve a problem with language, although not as Doughty meant it. Perhaps I can put it this way. It's possible to think of language as the most versatile, and maybe the original, form of deception, a sort of fortunate fall: I lie and am lied to, but the result of my lie is mental leaps, memory, knowledge.

196
We got up and wandered across the square, looking at some acrobats and musicians, but as soon as one of the performers spotted us as tourists, he would rush over to demand money before we had even seen anything. We tried to watch a snake charmer who was holding a snake by the neck a few inches from his mouth, almost licking it with his tongue, while an assistant was beating a drum. He spotted us and right away came over for money. We gave him a 50 francs piece which he looked at with disdain. He brought over a snake and asked us to touch it. It felt strangely cool and smooth in spite of the slight roughness of its tiny scales. It would bring us good luck, he said. We gave him a 100 franc piece, whereupon with an unpleasant grin he hung the snake around poor Edwin's neck, stroking its head, saying that it would make him rich and always keep him out of trouble with the police. I gave him another 100 francs so he would take the snake off Edwin's neck and before he could put it around mine, we fled.

78
Friday 12th.
Eating cherries today in front of the mirror I saw my idiotic face. Those self-contained bullets disappearing down my mouth made it look looser, more lascivious and contradictory than ever. It contains many elements of brutality, calm, slackness, boldness and cowardice, but as elements only, and it is more changeable and characterless than a landscape beneath scurrying clouds. That's why so many people find it so impossible to retain (You've too many of them, says Hedda).

137
6 Oct.
Since I arrived in Paris, there isn't a day that goes by that I don't window-shop in the bookstores. Sometimes I even go in to look through the shelves of books on display. And bit by bit I am feeling a profound distaste for literature. I don't really know what its origin is. Is it the enormous number of books that are appearing, the thousands of novels translated from every language, and somewhat at random (for Eça de Queiroz, Pio Baroja, Rebreanu, etc., are still unknown?) Complete anarchy, chaos. And the artificial production of the "new wave." This

too: a novel no longer interests the modern critic unless it's difficult, almost unreadable; or unless it illustrates a new theory of the novel or literature.

100

The cliché that clichés are cliché only because their truth is self-evident would seem self-evident. Yet from birth we're taught that things are not simple as they seem. The wise man's work is to undo complications: things are simple, truth blazes ("brightness falls from the air"), and the obvious way to prevent wars is not to fight. Thus, when I proclaim that I am never less alone than when I am by myself, and am met with a glazed stare, the stare is from one who abhors a vacuum—the look of nature. But I am complicating matters.

106

Yesterday I tried to let myself go completely. The result was that I fell into a deep sleep and experienced nothing except a great sense of refreshment, and the curious sensation of having seen something important while I was asleep. But what it was I could not remember; it had gone forever.

But today this pencil will prevent my going to sleep. I dimly see certain strange images that seem to have no connection with my past; an engine puffing up a steep incline dragging endless coaches after it. Where can it all come from? Where is it going? How did it get there at all?

13

Jean Jacques Rousseau confesses himself. It is less a need than an idea.

46

What tense would you choose to live in?
I want to live in the imperative of the future passive participle — in the "what ought to be."

I like to breathe that way. That's what I like. It suggests a kind of mounted, bandit-like equestrian honor...

FORREST GANDER

•　　　•　　　•

A MACULA OF LIGHT

Geometric Losses

never so much as. An oblique angle. Primitive oath, blood horizon. Her light cholera and one hundred more questions. The dreamt achievement of scorpions at audience. In the furrow weeds. Then double combs her hair. Pall bearer's vintage. When the bird begins alone the light. Its steady fillip into drain. Similarly but later, directed against telephone pole, its pizzle's hard pulse. Absence propped in her chair to preach. Critical orchestra. Low man among stinging arachnids grips the spade. *Dawn's on him*

Violence's Narrative Continued

Didn't he have a loincloth over his gentiles. And Goody's Headache Powder. Objects in mirror are closer than they appear. Disconnected last thoughts. Between the white center lanes a large red stain. Ascension Parrish. In the shaggy tree lodges one hubcap. The radio song finished. Without the driver. I attend Gloryland Baptist Church bumpersticker. Visible. On the bumper. Impaled on the bridge rail. Remember, someone had joked, rubber side down. In humid air the wheels each freely spinning Who's going to tell?

*The soft spot in the floor wakes him.

Meditative

A dog manages to catch its own tail. At first
the traveller laughs, but then shouts and weeps. No
news will ever be obtained regarding that
about to be lost.

Rain for forty days. Surrounded by mountains.
When it brims, the water has raised
him to the peak.

The responses to death are sometimes funny.
A man opens his wrist without drawing blood;
a woman opens a book with nothing inside.

JULIE KALENDEK

TAKE FIVE OF THESE

I am so tired of having a body
she said, buried up to the neck
to deny the misled forays deep in sand.

How much can I say when coming
from another state my bed is made.

Somatic myth. My life a string
pulled taut at one end.

—

For almost a week I kept
my thoughts tame. I would lean
into him. But you are my January
thirst, I would say. Convalescing.

He said, I broke my vow.

I knew how to let it work
from the inside out.

—

It was my absolute conviction.
The gesture was conclusive.

But I cut the air with scissors
positive of rigging, thin
invisible wires.

So mortally did I fear the sin
and weakness of presumption.

—

Her hands are at her temples.
When she cannot think of the word
her fingers fall and flutter birds.

Which stirs a sort of breeze
against her cheeks.

She looks confused.
She can't speak.

—

Once in existence. The body's demands.

We touch our head and then our heart
shoulder and shoulder, using one hand.

As with all non-sexual relationships
it was only at certain points in the
arc of the pendulum that I
could no longer ask.

—

I said
I'm looking for the secret. The key-
hole knot in the wood. The weak spot.
Some sputter of suffocation.

The children inside me are
dropping egg by egg.

Find something missing.

—

These are my fingers.
Unmanageable elegy.

    We breathe just enough. We take
    perhaps too little and forget.

Lack has a gorgeous advantage.

These are my fingers. I think
There are too many.

TOM MANDEL

THE ACTOR

Somber and hermetic, but approachable and of a divertingly theoretical bent, he was able to play all parts that were suited to him, and all were. Like a piano, he was able to play the violin part easily. Yet, a truly great actor is no mere musical instrument. Unambiguous, a train, he rumbles past the audience (sidecars).

Photography is an issue, because light paints its surfaces with a dream of dots. A thought that hid in his heart plunged him into heaven.

Action (thesis/murder). Blood (reaction). Diagnosis (synthesis /death). I'd say he finds himself inside an interesting rectangle.

OF BIRDS

The analyst of birds
birds storm through his windows
stars twist in his nerves

heaven hears his dismal mind
blink with thought

a dark wood bursts from
his ground in all directions

among gray trees that surround him

comes arching the narrow
beast to engage him.

GALE NELSON

• • •

from: *stare decisis*

Row after row (this
goes on for awhile)

of perfectly-
spaced stalks   (corn)

You left   (   )
so I can

See in   order
each

shared by
row after   row

I   am   too

    small   to

                fit on   the same
        canvas

          as my subject

          I relegate
        one
   then   the

other   reaching   linen   napkins
                          without
   design   if hair grew   on   my

              back   would
   I eat   more
              fiber
      last   ink

                wasted
on signatures

STEPHEN RODEFER

•   ••

INSCRIPTION

THE DAY WAS NEARLY FINISHED drawing clothes, and dusk was getting darker, slowing down all the ground hogs, and I was alone but I felt like engraving the evening anyway, a little sore I guess, but remembering that nothing really could go wrong and feeling like telling everyone just such a thing as this.

Help me to brainstorm this real idea and we'll both survive. If you've ever written a plan, give me a chance to break down the court and it'll all pass off. Don't give me any load about the past. I experience the present well enough, and don't need another deal beyond a few hands. I choose you for my toast and salve the entrance.

My going this way may be foolish — I'll leave the knowledge to you and your sense of it. As one who steals what he wills to change his mind, I make myself an ocean beside this dim coast, so I can quit what I have begun alone. This shady soul thus forges toward your ear like a false beast carrying cucumbers, stuffed with dynamite.

I intend to free you from hesitation. I'm going to tell you why we are here. I used to be in the dark about everything, then I just switched the toggle to the other position, and there was a woman standing in her language. Well, I had to speak so I said

> Oh gargantuan sister. Friend more potential than fortune. You're going to make it all be in time, aren't you. It's fascinating, though I got up late, but you're still here and I mean it. Neither speech nor escape could keep me from consolation. I will be truth if I come from desire, and it is light actually, now that I speak of this.

Grateful but not wanting to make any plans, she stood there still, the explanation of a wish. I wanted to know the cause, like any gradual, why she refused to come down into the center of this place, which was burning from one of the previous returns. I'll tell you, she said, I am not afraid. The only thing to fear is injury. The outside does not touch me. I warn you, I cannot be warmed except by warmth itself. I will be the enemy of cruelty, but I will still be cruel, but it will be pragmatism, even when the crowd can't figure out why they are miserable.

After she said this, she left. Which made me move toward the vacuum she had been fixing. A hefty sound, as of vented desire, came down on the side of a mountain, which lay still between its peaks. Little flowers huddled in behind the chilly night, erecting their safety with their stems. A faint closure, daring words to cease, disposed desire to go out in search of purpose again. The traveller decided to propose all will was one, even though the savage way was right and arduous. Greatness of stock sprang from hope to be nearer the ground, whatever the span. Weak sight could explain symbolical position only from a vantage beneath the earth.

Up in the air, the scintillation of the argyll lands below showed the passage proposed on earth to be a violent fraud. The faithful spherical remove was a great advantage, equating vitamin with mineral, laughter with forgetting.

Of course the straight way was to be lost, the hard thing to be wild. And realizing the goal was in the middle could bear the proof and basically renew thought, which everyone wanted. I'll read you all about it after this.

MARJORIE WELISH

••   •

RESPECTED, FEARED, AND SOMEHOW LOVED

In the long run we must fix our compass,
and implore our compass,
and arraign our shadow play in heaven, among the pantheon
where all the plea-bargaining takes place.
                                      Within the proscenium arch,
the gods negotiate ceaselessly,
and the words he chooses to express the baleful phrase
     dare to be obsessed
with their instrumentality. Please send for our complete catalogue.

As in the days of creation, the clouds gossip and argue,
     the gods waver.
The gods oversee such unstable criteria as fourthly, fifthly.
The rest are little timbral touches.
The gods waver. To reiterate a point, the gods oversee
the symposium on the life raft — a crazed father, a dead son;
                               an unwarranted curtailment of family.

Part of the foot, and thus part of the grace splinter in dismay,
and the small elite of vitrines where our body parts are stored
dies in a plane crash in Mongolia.
Why didn't someone do something to stop the sins of the climate,
                                         and earlier,

why did not someone rewrite the sins of the vitrines, the windows
shipwrecked icily, the windows called away?

VEIL

An enchanted frame assures the image of a loved one.
Then there is the question of response.
A loved one produces things. Then there is this question
of existence.
                        Motion, dashed to the ground,
and now a hapless pattern in its stead.
Little portions of liveliness are thrown out as inquiries.

Then there is the day that lives up to its preconceived ideas.
Then there is the day
empowered to train all sense on the moment,
holding onto that bias, often and later,
                                although meanwhile,
the day is in position and has empowered the senses
to caress the starstruck flames,
the excited jets surrounding these inquiries.

                                If there is a pattern
of stars beyond the starstruck blue, it spells desire,
and beyond this, a paler tendency
for stars to sift a desire to be anywhere, and you
not even among them in question form.

BLOOD OR COLOR

Across a room,
a handshake in a late, large design
has caught the overflow of the heart, the human figure as a source.
"Have you sent me my bouquet of gladiolus?" the poet asks.
"No, I haven't," I say, "but I have emphasized it."

Across a room, a writer queries,
"Have you reached my claim check and my watercolors,
    have you introduced a bouquet of gladiolus?"
"No," I say, compressed in ambiguous space,
"but I have brought you your bouquet of gladiators."

"No," I say,
"but as in the arena of this room,
interrogation is impaled on intimacy: gladiators burst
and metamorphose into the womanly bright remains of our city."

This pediment forfeits nothing; these gladiolus are inextinguishable.
The most brilliant blue eyes obtained by natural means
flare as if in a greeting, herd or flock.
A herd or flock is numerically great.
Is this my gift: the human figure pierced and confessed?
But the sky had altered:

Pierced and splashed, and driven
like the arena of command
drives the volume, line and light
of rooms we enter,

here is a man, some victory;
some victory, though not all of it,
some victory with outstretched arm
like Alexander,

the marble face
with hurtful tools at the deepest level.
"They are afraid of you.
That's why they are so obsequious."

JEAN DAIVE

•• •

EDEN

A woman measures.

A woman opens her arms
to determine lengths or
proportions.

She values
the sleep of this man who
will never sleep again.

You must know
everything begins
with the enlargement
photographically
of a
comma.

Which
makes a sound.

A sudden
slowing,
liquid against light
for this photograph
through the fog.

That which you see is composed
of a man and woman
entirely.

The chair. Sitting in the corner.
You are alone in the room. You smoke
perhaps, your knees against your chin.

Still alone
you enter
the
noise of the street.

You see blue shadows
running past
and in the eyepiece
flesh.

An interruption of words
through the fog.

A rosy scent
drifts
around the house.

The garden
burns.

A stone drops
and you are no longer heavy.

The end outlined
as in the story of a passion.

But a kinetic sense of the world is avoided.

And the need for separation
is recovered.

Your chair
also
is it not linked
to what the author would say?

You smile. Note a disconnection.

What forestalls
the hesitation,
a system of coordinates?

the world of a long,
long film
does not protect you.

Because
that world is not the one
to which your eyes are accustomed.

It is the end of the day.
The end of subtitles.

The dark is dustless
like women.

The smoke surges
sideways
through the frame
like a pulse.

Later.

Exhaustion in the room and in
the bed, time is ill-begotten.

translated from the French by Julie Kalendek

ELIZABETH MACKIERNAN

•   •   •

from: *ANCESTORS MAYBE*

IT WAS IN THE MONTH OF BRAMBLE THAT THINGS BEGAN TO HAPPEN.

"Bramble is like that," says Marie Madeleine hopefully, "the equinoctial winds and all. Things are bound to change."

Marie Madeleine takes an interest in the sciences. The science she takes the most interest in is, of course, magic.

"I know the Irish word for bramble," says Marie Celeste, "but I have temporarily forgotten it. I'm sure it begins with an M."

Marie Celeste is devoted to the languages of Europe. Of all the languages of Europe, Irish is the one most easily forgotten. . . unless it is Welsh.

"Perhaps tomorrow I will decorate the house for Bramble," says Marie Angelique. "I will weave briars and bittersweet all around the railings and paint a picture of wind on the garage door."

Marie Angelique is an artist. She is quite capable of painting a picture of wind. Her inner picture of it is quite clear — even overpowering.

No one should be surprised that the sisters are all named Marie.

It is the month of Bramble but nothing much seems to be happening. The sisters go on living in Middletown, Connecticut. They mark off the days on the tree calendar. Perhaps the tree calendar does not quite fit the seasons of Connecticut. But no one will ever admit that.

TOWARD THE END OF BRAMBLE THE SISTERS BEGAN TO STUDY HERALDRY.

"First the potato famine and now this," said the mournful Mr. O'Nolan when he heard the news.

115

The Science of Heraldry. The Art of Heraldry. The Language of Heraldry.

"As for the language of heraldry," says Marie Celeste, "it is very amusing. It is almost one of the languages of Europe."

She makes careful notes on the vocabulary and syntax of blazonry. The colors of heraldry are: Gules, Azure, Vert, Sable and Purpure. In heraldry adjectives come after nouns. There are many participles but no verbs.

These are the traditional arms of the sisters:
Ermine, two lions passent gules.

Marie Celeste's brain is one of those brains that shifts into dialect without any planning. This can be viewed as either a strange and wonderful talent or a peculiar neurological handicap. She looks out the window and sees the house next door (it is the professor's house) against a blue sky with an airplane flying by.

"Vert," she thinks, "a house statant proper on a chief azure an airplane volant argent."

BE CAREFUL, MARIE CELESTE, A DIALECT WITHOUT VERBS LEAVES YOUR MIND STANDING STILL AND STARING.

"A griffin, I can understand," says Marie Madeleine. "A demi-griffin, for instance, can always be distinguished from a demi-eagle by the ears. But what in the world is a wyvern???"

Marie Angelique draws heraldic devices. She even uses a compass to get things symmetrical. It is a new experience for her to be interested in symmetry. She is generally interested in wild profusion and riots of detail. She shows her sisters a picture of a wyvern — a sort of dragon with wings and only two legs. Ordinary dragons have four legs plus or minus wings. Angels also have two arms plus wings but that is another problem.

Marie Madeleine finds a reference to a place called Ormskirk.
"Ormskirk?" she asks in amazement, "Worm church?"
"Dragon church, really," says Marie Celeste.

Marie Celeste has begun to study calligraphy. People who are devoted to the study of grammar frequently are attracted to letters as well. She has learned to write an elegant hand...when she remembers to do so.

Marie Madeleine and Marie Angelique are amazed. Suddenly Celeste's notes which previously have been full of blots and scrawls begin to look like pages torn from the Book of Kells.

She still leaves them lying about the house. Some habits change, but not all at once.

Dr. Sandwich visits the sisters from time to time to discuss the lunar calendar.

Marie Celeste tells him once again. "When the month of Ivy ends the month of Reed begins."

Dr. Sandwich does not remember things like that very well. Dr. Sandwich finds it very convenient that the sisters are all named Marie.

Marie Madeleine reads in the paper that a dragon has been seen in the skies over Hartford, Connecticut, flying low over the Russian Orthodox dome of the gun factory — a blue dome sprinkled with golden stars.

Naturally it is some sort of hoax. A balloon, perhaps, or a very large kite.

THERE IS NOT NOW NOR COULD THERE EVER BE A PLACE CALLED ORMSKIRK IN THE STATE OF CONNECTICUT. (DON'T FORGET TO BREATHE, MARIE ANGELIQUE.)

Marie Celeste stops listening. She is thinking about the Russian word pravoslavniy.

Marie Madeleine also reads in the paper that there is a danger of drought. Forest fires are predicted for the State of Connecticut. Someone has copied onto a scrap of paper a spell that begins

"Wyrm com snican......"

"Is that a spell for rain?" wonders Marie Madeleine, "Or something else?"

HUGO CONTINUES TO LIVE WITH THE SISTERS. THEY HAVE NEVER DOUBTED HIS GENIUS.

One evening in the month of Ivy Dr. Sandwich appears at the door. He has just come from the zoo. Dr. Sandwich identifies with elephants. Coming into the house, he makes lumbering noises and swings his massive head. There is a smell of stampede in the air. Professor Davenport who has come over from next door begins to feel nervous, but Marie Celeste is not alarmed. She's seen this mood before.

"In the Bois de Boulogne...," begins the doctor, and stares off into space swaying gently from side to side.

Hugo offers to make the tea. Dear Hugo.

Dr. Sandwich usually appreciates the dark honey which the sisters are in the habit of stirring into their tea. For the moment, however, he is unable to hold a spoon. He has forgotten about his hands.

"Are you familiar with the word 'skep'?" asks Marie Celeste, just to change the subject. "It is an old-fashioned bee-hive."

Marie Angelique imagines it means 'ship'. With her artist's eye she sees a tiny crew of honey bees sailing a golden craft. Honey drips from the yard-arms. The queen lounges below deck.

"When winter comes," she says, "the drones will walk the plank — but not yet."

Dr. Sandwich stares at Marie Angelique in alarm.

Marie Celeste begins to read aloud from the Bible. The Bible is known to have a calming effect. The Bible she picks up happens to be in Swedish, a language her sisters can almost understand. Hugo, being a genius, understands it perfectly. He is happy to learn that Samson is called Simson in Swedish.

Da föll Herrens Ande över honum, och han slet sönder lejonet, såsom hade han slitet en killing, fastän han icke hade någonting i sin hand. En tid därefter vände han tillbaka och vek då av vägen för att se på det döda lejonet; då fick han i lejonets kropp se en bisvärm med honung.

Dr. Sandwich does not understand a word of Swedish, but he has dozed off anyway.

Marie Celeste puts down the Swedish Bible. "The terrible part comes later," she says.

IT IS NOT SAFE TO ASSUME THAT HUGO IS A DWARF. HE MAY STILL BE GROWING.

IT IS NOT TRUE THAT THE SISTERS ARE UNEMPLOYED. THEY ARE CONSULTANTS.

On Hallowe'en (they call it Samhain when they remember to do so) the three sisters dress up as three brothers. All wear small dark mustaches and old-fashioned trousers tucked into black boots. Everyone is out walking on Hallowe'en night. The sisters stamp their feet and snap their fingers and laugh in low rumbling tones.

At the top of the street near the grassy knoll they run into Professor Davenport. He is dressed as his ancestor, the Cavalier, tonight. He sweeps off his hat with the ostrich plume and bows extravagantly to the sisters.
"Ah," he says with a giggle, "Shadrach, Meshach and Abednego, I presume."

The sisters go on their way. "For a minute I thought he was the Garter King of Arms," says Marie Celeste, "but naturally not."

Marie Madeleine frowns. Was Celeste criticizing the professor? She dislikes it when her sisters speak disparagingly of Professor Davenport. After all, despite appearances, he is her husband.

Marie Angelique asks a young woman to dance. It is Josephine dressed as Maid Marion. Josephine frequently dresses as Maid Marion. It is odd that no one in America ever dresses as Robin. Marie Angelique and Josephine whirl about in the moonlight. Dried leaves fly up in the air.

Marie Madeleine buys small skeletons made out of sugar. Everyone is eating bones tonight.

Should they have left the doors unlocked tonight? Should they have set out food for the spirits? There is a certain risk. Today is the day of the dead.

Someone is singing that old song. . . The King of Spiral Castle Is Leaving for the War.

MARIE CELESTE, DON'T BE DISTRESSED. A SINGLE BAD DREAM DOES NOT MAKE A WORLD.

The days grow rapidly shorter. Marie Madeleine does not have much time to study the science of Heraldry. She rides the bus to Hartford every day. She walks past the municipal building and the two stone lions look back at her. "Soyez sages, pussycats," she whispers.

Marie Madeleine has been working as a consultant for one of the giant insurance companies of Hartford for several years. Now she is designing information systems.

It frequently occurs to her that someone has made a mistake.

IN THE PINK OF THE EARLY MORNING THE BLESSED MOTHER LEFT HER NICHE IN THE WALL. ON TINY PLASTER FEET SHE STEPPED AMONG THE DEAD LEAVES LOOKING FOR SOMETHING.

HUGO WATCHED HER FROM AN UPSTAIRS WINDOW. IF HE WAS SUR-PRISED HE DIDN'T SHOW IT.

Meanwhile Dr. Sandwich has taken up roller-skating.

"Oh, Dr. Sandwich, it is not a good idea to roller-skate here where the leaves are falling so fast!"

Marie Celeste helps the doctor to his feet. He lurches wildly and continues on his way.

SOON ANOTHER WONDERFUL THING WILL BE HAPPENING. INTERESTING AT LEAST, IF NOT REALLY WONDERFUL.

RAY RAGOSTA

• • •

AT THE COAST

Words shipwreck upon ecstasy, yet are
unable to navigate the shoals of discourse.
Memory moves into fog
and takes human form.

Though propositions are scrupulously set forth,
syllables split in the ear,
like wood,
disquisition founders.
Silence grows molten.

Pinched optic disquiet of the figure's
drifting, as seated, then standing,
till consuming passion cools:
Questions are too large and don't fit;
sources of information wash up in the wrong places.

EXCURSIONS

A kind of malignant mind creeps through earth,
lit only by the light of the movies.
Facts reversed will not clear the atmosphere or escape
into the crevices of memory.
Not that all this is foul, but itinerant.
A poverty limits our excursions,
for to go begging at the four corners
would inevitably land us in jail,
with its attendant universals,
dark, dampness, long constraint, which evidence
keen understanding of human nature
with its spots, wrinkles, pestilent beginnings.
Only so many notes act as departures,
leaving more order than can be reckoned with.

BRITA BERGLAND

• • •

UP YONDER IN THE MEADOW OF CHILDREN

There are
in the back of the mind
molted graces
ladies courtesy a
store window. These
inviting mores
more or less
are children of my age
regrettably
pitched and purloined.
Not with golden custody
the animal kingdom as
little purple sweatshirts
live in two states, share
a common zipcode.
The child is split
or a bridge.

Suppose you lie down flat
in the square
where the traffic is heaviest
you're eating a chocolate croissant
your daughter is in ballet class
you're over there
somewhere in Claremont
on the fourth floor of a furniture
store. On a bed
there's an axe and you start
chopping at legs.
It's not serious
this one thing or another
you lie back down.

Take 20 questions.
Animal vegetable mineral
arrogance nor there
hot pastrami, fritos, orange pop
each little bite a delicious
end in itself
or bludgeoned by a fire extinguisher
the land is a refrain defamed
for the dead-at-head, or heart,
I'm not sure which.

PAM REHM

•• •

THUS I FIND MY LEGS

I.

Where does your body enter alleviating the wait of the test I must make of my body?

The feeling, of course, is not wanting and a hope that this feeling is enough. It is only the time. Present.

Needing outside assurance is the difficulty that exposes the process. While chemical, the psychological is largely involved. For the proliferation is equal to nothing we can explain. In full.

Other indicators eventually limit movement. Like the bullfrog's throat that becomes round. Its bellow, another occupation for hearing.

Apprehension is an inability the feet make of themselves.

The apprehension they make of us.

Decide to wait for God and later decide not to brings about a stop and that's why pain enters in. Needing a suffering. Just in case a truth is revealed.

We are paying for all of this unnecessary construction. Knowing this hasn't seemed to move us into devotion or out onto the missile fields. We are afraid. To act.

Or are too young to consider ourselves older. As in sitting in a chair, breasts exposed.

II.

There is a hidden sense of. Hiding.

There is also a deadened potential.

There is a barbed wire fence. Or other to keep out what one doesn't want to get in. For one the fence is mystery. For a second, the fence keeps us out of the capability to destruct. Thirdly, the fence stops us from expanding before want.

There is an apprehension because there is also betrayal.

The halt, in spite of past frustrations, is we don't know if this is the place from which solutions will come.

The halt is wanting an excuse, and more importantly, the specifics.

III.

As sure as the heat was not there to warm us, we subverted the feeling of missing each other.

The absence of heat is affected by the brain's need to have something else to think about.

We sometimes remember that heat is the subject of our desire and abandon it. But eventually our own heat overwhelms us.

IV.

The fact of sex under a microscope can be determined beforehand.

I have, on the other hand, an apprehension as to what exists outside of myself. As force. Thus, my waiting isn't spoiled.

There is no loss of speed. My decision to not know comes from my inability to affirm the prediction.

I remember the needle swinging above my mother's wrist read as one boy and four girls. However, he is absent.

I could never ask if he had existed because I was never told the story. Sometimes I thought that I only overheard myself.

V.

I tried to make my apprehension into a past betrayal. I could not stand, however. Straight.

What I had was not a vision of. Precisely.

Sometimes nothing inside me was apprehension. Other times it was emptiness and want.

As the motion becomes more disordered things become less stationary. I thought we too would become vertebrae for other things.

Instead our tasks consumed us. Round glasses for reading ourselves to sleep.

What I wanted was less supposing. But this was not a need.

A chair is less myself than wooden floor. Thus, I find my legs. Underneath me.

CLAIRE NEEDELL

•   • •

NOT A BALANCING ACT

My departure made the leaves gather more quickly
and there were twenty odd dogs and these were
also leaves. I wonder if it is not my own
anticipation which abets that formation,
I wonder if it is not a sense more primordial
than fear: a scent, a neural output. If a person
feels afraid another person is in a costume. His interest
in a clean sink is a particular type of footnote.
Now I await the want of silence. This is
the equivalent of taking note of a branch on fire.
It doesn't happen in the movies. It is not what
is happening now. In fact I walk around the table
and I can tell by looking at him my eyes abide no
geometrical principle. The front of the house,
I have discovered, leans a little to the left.
But the door which glistens and is red is absolutely
central.

———

If I am wearing lipstick, or jewelry, I am kept warm,
as though I were standing close to the body
of a horse. If atypical shapes are encountered
one may recall the flawed concept of phrenology.
This may or may not be a woman's head. So there
must be more light. She seems concerned again
with forming a course of conduct. There is no
metaphor for this, one simply walks, and when no
sign manifests itself, that nakedness has an
astonishing simplicity. And nothing will be
asked of it.

———

The house is dug into the side of a hill, so it truly
looks like nothing more than a mound of earth. She has
many idealized visions as to the fundamental nature of the
body, of environs, some of which seem probable and
some of which might provide comfort. The children hide
within yellow trash barrels, and have given names
to various caves. A car is a cave and a hotel is a
cave. Since one never has the proper angle, a person
may be observed, but giving a name to any event is a
matter of pure inference. She sees a pictograph and no
picture. So she enjoys the feeling of being pregnant
but will resist giving birth.

———

It occurs to me that nothing may be unusual.
I can't tell by looking at the sky that this
is the holiday season. He has spent all of his
cash. The cat fits into the palm of my hand,
and is invalid. Any purchase is motivated
by an emotion. All my new clothing contains suet
and seed. He will not say "I am dying to touch you".
Even as I pound my chest, I realize this —
Display more significant than offering —
Or the natural attitude of a bottle —
This is as if I cannot be.
A feeling of personal abandonment pervades
even the abstract,   there is no birthplace
so there is no melodrama,

He just stands that way. He is not posing
like a curtain.

———

I offer to turn on my side so my mother can
see me better. I am facing him again and he
might as well be smoking a cigar. I wish
he would put on a play. That way, I too, could
be gratified by the way he thinks of only one
thing at a time. Even when one sees a hero
barefoot, one will inevitably focus on his
chin. This is not a real pregnancy. It is just
that I am the only woman in the whole train station.
The darkness outside is identical to the darkness
underground. My body does not actually differ
from his. So I must keep explaining my sex, insistent
that it is not temporary.

———

If the scent of wood is strong, the trip takes on
the atmosphere of exodus. An omen or premonition
alleviates the feeling of labor. Since speed is also
a necessity, the appearance of a single object cannot
be sustained. She wishes she could see a spider
come out of hiding, a leg of light. Her black glasses
are a remark on the translucence of the sexual act.
The antler grows its points and then is seasonally shed.
Likewise, rapture can be a form of detritus. The mist
is not rain but an emanation. The way his voice enlarges
the socket of her eye, but not the eye itself. When the
body is, as they say "inflamed by passion", the skull
is a former location. When darkness falls the steeple
is reinvented as an electric wire. In this way her
departure from him is constant, but he —

he discontinues.

SERIE d'ECRITURE No. 7

•••

Anne Portugal •

that actual day
I saw the sky at hand
gardens like this
later

on the back of the stone bench
you write your contribution to the story of the little dog

the dog was very interesting to me
    its girth
    the two bridges
    over the Seine and over the Eure

the dog was very interesting to me
    stay you askew
    the boat you did not have
    you will cross only once

the dog was very interesting to me
    its girth
    toward which
    the arched bridge leads

it is not nothing being this dog
    red on the front
    and blue
    to the ears

what will be
the following experience

the merging of heavenly bodies

an effort of intensity
thick
as air

visibly your foot
fixed
and your lateral thumbs

could not contain
raised
emotion when it changes to pain

we have seen that places on earth generally
corked
and when one is inside

divert from the subject of air

and in order to notice you
it is the last of things
they have thought

that you were balanced in the air

translated from the French by Norma Cole

Dominique Grandmont •
from: *DOWN HERE*

I

but the sun point-blank (the very air massacred by the blink of an eye) all faces all of a sudden the same one way or the other time always like a ray of light under the door

•

sea caved in frayed blur of a very dim moon and trucks madly bearing down on the stars while blood already covered us all in warm vines

•

well-springs: stairs (and thorns: windows) where is there freedom in the world?

•

what wall to hear bees pour their flaming honey into cellars this lamp in bright day equidistant from light and dark

•

opening the clockwork of a vein (photos taken on floors of sky in a building under construction) he howled so loud it was hard to believe him alive

•

and the fear if he opens his mouth he'll remember almost all (or else wake them up even tell them to lie because nothing is beautiful enough for them to take in how true their words)

translated from the French by Rosmarie Waldrop

Dominique Fourcade •
MURAL

Des mots sur un plan
Pour qu'il se change en espace
Parce que les mots sont de l'espace (ainsi les mots je t'aime donnent son
   volume à l'amour et le mot ciel ses hectares au lieu entre les parois de
   l'arche tandis que
La passe du mot nuage — consonnes et voyelles — décide de sa beauté
   de son drame
Un quatuor — le mot rose — spacieux et mental s'il en est — fonde le mot
   existence)
Et parce que l'espace est de première nécessité sur la blessure
Oui
L'espace comme lumière

Paul Green
MORAL

Dour smuts, or unplanned
poor callers, each hinge on a space
by schools; mutes and dolls, poisons, oils, mortars, jetting down in
   sun-flame. All are mortal, or morsel. So, as actors, all are on trails.
   Parade, larch, town, disk;
loops dumped near jerking suns. It fails, dies; or dead-easy beauty dies,
   in drama,
ink, water, lime; a tree's spaces owe torment. All's a lonest fund, limit,
   or cursed tense;
a torpor's sequels. Poor sister, prim, or nicest; syllables are
 where
less pass. Come, lay me here.

Isabelle Hovald •
STELE FOR LENZ

> *"...he had lost the end of his sentence; at which point he
> thought it necessary to keep hold of the last word spoken
> and to talk without stopping..."* —G. Büchner, *Lenz*

He'd come to me from worlds deep down and settled in the dust,
arriving at the dark door (wind threading the trees with their unceasing
trembling) to slip suddenly through the hinges —

moaning O

He'd not reach me, his steps on the gravel, the door slammed to in the
afternoon, my head up, listening —

that still shock of an embrace

———

At that moment I'd recall the town when we came; having spent years
there I failed to recognize it. Fatigue pulsed in our temples, entering by
every fiber, every fissure, the body exhausted, weak, sleep-shaken, winded.

Nothing would have happened between leaving for the mountains January
20, our going through town (his looking haggard), and the discovery of the
body ("his body was found in a street in Moscow in the year 17—").

Nothing. Nevertheless, I will always think of that sudden darkening,
how the expression in a face, in the eyes, was tarnished (and of the effort
to dissimulate with an unmeaning smile).

———

As for him, coming farthest, most foreign to this land, he may attend my haunting, which will remain outside my comprehension
— so dangerous where he was coming from —

Was it a matter, here again, of passion, thwarted as we had been

pursuing courageously (and he kept hold of me)

——

Pursuing, the jot of things I never knew, of things not visible, of things my brother, my lover never wrote to me.

I will see only this haste in winter, and the secret,

The stele forever cracked in separation, and under my hand the stone, rough but without epitaph, inscription sought which would give nothing away

this fragment of breath in the mouth's mourning, the throbbing echo of a Lied.

——

Would remain:

The face of one forever dying, inexpressive, unimaginable agony which will bring me endlessly these images, this scene.

and
at close of afternoon, plains running under the sky, the heavy motion of leaves before a rain:
raised up askew the stone (phrase suspended, interrupted, with the coming of the forgotten, the unpublished, the invented) shadow already

dark on the grass between tilted facets, you still walked before me, face turned towards the fog climbing the mountain you came from

would remain:

hair lifted from time to time by the wind. He had had to collapse, they had had to find him there, self-forgotten, his hair, heedless, blowing.

———

The death of Lenz has not taken place,

was it I, the mountain, the car that brought him back to the plain, towards the town, or winter in a distant country.

He, the one passing, he, the crossing of his own passage — and who can be, only in being absent, his stele.

Stele, thrown down, suppliant space, space of elegy for want of this intimate death, no one is buried here.

Would remain: the motion of interment, opening an earth into which we can put nothing, which we cannot reclose, marking the polished stone with loss, with obliteration.

translated from the French by Keith Waldrop

PAOL KEINEG

• •   •

from: *BOUDICA*

> Boudica, with her daughters before her in a chariot, went up to tribe
> after tribe, protesting that it was indeed usual for Britons to fight under
> the leadership of women. "But now," she said, "it is not as a woman
> descended from noble ancestry, but as one of the people that I am
> avenging lost freedom, my scourged body, the outraged chastity of my
> daughters. Roman lust has gone so far that not our very persons, nor
> even age or virginity, are left unpolluted. But heaven is on the side of a
> righteous vengeance; a legion which dared to fight has perished; the
> rest are hiding themselves in their camp, or are thinking anxiously of
> flight." —Tacitus, *Annals XVI*

1

Over the testicles of bulls, over the seven pigeon-stained saints, greetings
to those who wither in this narrow place.

Between birth and death, between Shell and Esso: force-fed with
metaphysics, with cultural affairs, with total staging.

The wonder revolves. Atop the cliff, the parking lot and the field of
gravel. This quarrelsome land, curbed and pumped.

The January rain a hundred thousand times over. Periphery and the
Law. We detach our words, speaking only in dreams.

2

From the sacred wood to bitter fiefdoms, a crowd of minor characters. In
the sleepy hinterland, gastric troubles, ancestral slumber.

The people adore this mountain. Throne, pedestal, indirect lighting.
God speaks to them in person, thermonuclear.

She presides at the opening session. Earth at quarter tilt.

It's my history piled to the ceiling, my burning beneficent anxiety.

Gaps in the landscape, and a particular way of playing the ass. Filthy countryside. The greaseballs our ears get stuffed with.

Four walls in the wind, and the weather reports. Lost in this manner, we remember the forest, we stretch out our sleep.

In the prison of the vaguely sacred tree. In the prison of air. Burning smile, silence in action.

Fear of wolves, the nightingale interrupting. Good stories that could. The impossible.

4

Geography of the colonizer, from the fenced-off land's end to the web of roads for wheat and tin. Desperadoes and reservists. The power-elite sub-prefect, the sub-prefect's wife as Winged Victory.

Colonizer's history, always passionate and blonde. O centuries of light, savages back to back, our own sweet will, divine right.

Everything happens if so. So so.

Tons of mud, the gods bamboozled.

5

Grammarian and philologist, in obscure periods. And if it were necessary to start over. Claiming a share in what's shaken up. Peeping Toms.

Pigs swim round in the cauldron. Voice paler than usual. Full speed ahead.

On bread and water. So many old words, so many foolhardy gestures. The blotter, sand.

A.D. 61, time of humiliations. The people who lay dormant are now on their feet. Heart racing, courage in spurts.

translated from the French by Keith Waldrop

FRIEDERIKE MAYRÖCKER

•   •   •

from: *SCHUBERT, OR: NOTES ON THE WEATHER, VIENNA*

1st Weather:

beside the sun, actually, and skinny enough to set on fire : lightning
in wing formation, you could feel the fish leap up in the brook.
Rapturous prose, to wit, 36 postillions blowing about, everyone's lovers.
And the lovers banded together and formed such societies punch bowl
full to the brim.

2nd Weather:

out of the corner of my eye I could see how he borrowed a typewriter
from the hotel clerk, belted it on like a vendor's tray and so squeezed into
the elevator, into his room.
Trickling away, spittoons filled with lavender. The other hotel guests con-
firmed, the resemblance was unmistakeable : plump placid *putto* body
brown curls graceful curve of lips eyes melancholy *Schubert glasses*
(which, it is claimed, he does not take off at night so as to note down
themes right on awakening or give way to feelings which, with scrolls
and flourishes in the old style, even *Dreimädchen* chocolates).
"Me:" Franz Schubert writes to Therese Grob, "will you ever come to
know me?"

3rd Weather:

while forced to wait out a downpour : that W. A. Rieder painted a water-
color of Schubert at a slight angle, dreamy, if not without pose.
Tongues tattling; shrill noon light.
Fortune's lap child caught in lightning; he should worry because he's
part of the band — the coach overturned.

4th Weather:

a *note* dressing him down, and he sighs in pitch. "That fire," Franz
Schubert writes to Therese Grob, "kindled in you *by circumstance.*"
"Like trickling when the box *slowly tore open* and my books tumbled out
on the floor while you danced and stomped your feet that the whole
room shook, yea heaven, and I nearly emptied the inkwell on my draft
instead of the sand."
"A pleasant opening of your eyes tomorrow morning."

5th Weather:

and reproaches himself, *groundswell.*
While some kinds of order / tones / descend, others rise; so that the
extreme poles of a stormy landscape draw together, former shrill
circumstances blur — a journey, on foot, to the Lobau.
Shoemaker's glass ball, a lamp, a shower.
Descriptive : white rivers in the gutter, in the puddles, reflections of
lightning; fishermen, Danube boatmen, strenuous laughs from the inn;
feelings that simply *tumble* over each other.

6th Weather:

"as if," Franz Schubert writes to Therese Grob, "the tongue *of my foot*
were torn out, by its tongue-root;"
"as if I wore, above my left ankle, on the outside of the leg, so that I could
feel it, a tattooed caduceus—"
and to brother Ferdinand: "*no sooner the baby* delivered! (Mass in B Flat)
than I'm swept off again, overwhelmed, utterly, unearthly, urgent, while
the last piece is only just being engraved..."
Tropical accompaniment, let it blow on me.
Out of the corner of my eye I could see how he got the telephone
directory from the hotel clerk; could follow his tongue as it whispered,
missing twice : "t'one directory... t'one directory!..." Could see him —
after much leafing through — absorbed in one of the volumes.

7th Weather:

plates of landscapes and instrumentalists, *from lead cuts.*
Wads of snow outside the window.
"Woke up at five this morning," Franz Schubert writes to Therese Grob,
"half frozen, on top of the bed with my clothes on."
"Too little modulation in places, and are you really letting these notes
which are lying about, these childish —"
and to his friend Schober : "as if they had eyes all over, those ladies,
scattered all over their skin, six-eighths. And their scant talent for
conversation — the darling statues! so vague and easily convincing. . ."

8th Weather:

what a bare morning!
painterly to the painters, at heavenly length!
in the thick of it, pancakes with sugar. Antiphonal choirs in black chalk on
blotting paper — the prompter's box would have the loudest word.
In the bushes, *drowned out,* singing.
"The geography of Salzburg," Franz Schubert writes to Therese Grob,
"all lost (Gastein). Where we nowhere remember ever having been."
"How can I thank you for not refusing my letters on a sad subject."

translated from the German by Rosmarie Waldrop

DAVID MILLER

• • •

IN THE FIELD

    1.

'don't turn away where are you gazing
and whatever are you gazing at?'
'there was a huge golden man'
the girl said 'lying down on a couch
and the couch was in a field'

    2.

details reproduced through layers levels
the dream coming home in day's hours

    3.

a line in vermilion
brushed onto paper
gold body-colour
anticipations of black
on white revealing birds
and immortal beings

    4.

'throughout that field there were outbursts
of crying' but the children take on the aspect
of celestial nymphs and a love
from before birth's remembered
unearthly life stirring in faces

5.

and the tribute which he offered
was a picture of the Lord of Heaven
and of the Mother of the Lord
altogether improper things he brought bones
of supernatural beings they are superfluous things
which ought not to enter the palace

6.

disseisin *where were we now*
where else could we be
than in that same field

BRIAN SCHORN

•• •

ENTERING POETIC BLINDSPOTS

What I am trying to say is this: from now on we must enter the poem from its blindspot. We must force ourselves into the danger of not seeing in order to see the poem more clearly, to see it as clearly as the head of a giant pin being thrust through the walls of the mouth. In other words, we might poke pins through our mouths in order to discipline ourselves not to speak, so that we can see ourselves go blind inside the meat of the poem. Understand this: the retina is a fool, having never said a thing. See the yellowing walls of the poem close in to speak to us, see our bodies say what we mean in a poem as we fall to the ground in total collapse of its presence. Let a fatal combustion take place at the core of the retina in order to explode it into a million pieces of useless abstraction. What a joy in the blindness of really seeing the poem at any point before it ever imagined itself in a word to see, to say this completely blind, to know this in the meat of the poem that will never come to the surface of the poem. So we enter from here now, completely naked, completely confused, completely poetic. We smile and accept that language is a futile attempt to see anything alive in a poem. We see poems dead. Yes, but O the life in a blindspot.

COLE SWENSEN

• ̥   •

CROWD

for Elizabeth Robinson

1

To love is to remove the face
Acres of day
God is a child who might
Break in a glance

Do it enough. Do it alone.
Say you'll go on
Like this

When I woke up I saw a road
And realized I'd been dreaming
Of New York — not of the city
But of the name on a map such
Disparity. And then I woke up
And saw a face. It wasn't
A specific face

"I have been sad for a long time."
He practiced the line again and again
There is nowhere
In the world that doesn't appear
On a map

The magnifying glass
In its leather case
Still on the windowsill

2

One should never die with
The hands empty they should
Be full of hands. One should never let one

And now something has happened to the throat

You must love God as you
Would a child. The hands so easily
Form a bowl and the face
In the water was no face
You knew

But we are changed so much by our bodies

And slowly turn the page

The water you hear running
Among this slow turning
Is something living
Where it can no longer breathe

You have to touch God just
Barely. The children playing
in the street are going blind
Bright flashes at the far edge
Of the cornea whole
At this speed

The heart is a machine

3

The heart is a measure a
Constant, count

The faces
Once
The gate of the face has been
Taken away

God is a fragile thing
That visits the body in fractured
Stories like maps of indivisible inhabitable
Territories like a child as you close the book says
Let's begin again

And now the heart cannot be
Found, blades
Of grass, a vagrant frame
You do but alone
And you aim it.

If the body were a country, a
Century and ice
The speaking made her sleepy
And she reached down not thinking

To take something up from the sand
It was a doll's head it would fit
In your hand the face
Erased by the surf, the unknown face and the hunch
Of a shape that is the heart
That is a hive with its relentless community.

DALLAS WIEBE

•   •   •

SKYBLUE'S ESSAY ON PUTTING NEW
SHOELACES IN YOUR SHOES

When a shoelace breaks, it is a moment of great discomfort and confusion. No one knows what to do when that happens. You can try to tie the two pieces of shoelace together, but that never works because the laces do not slide through the eyelets properly and one end of the lace is always too short to be tied in the bow at the top of the shoe. You can try to use the longest piece of lace and try to relace the shoes, but that doesn't work either because one end of the lace has no hard point and you have to lick it to get it through the eyelets. Again, too short. The only thing to do is to get a new pair to end the confusion and, if for no other reason, for the pleasure of lacing up again.

It makes you wonder why we don't carry an extra pair of shoelaces with us. We carry spare tires, extra dollars, extra handkerchiefs, spare umbrellas, Swiss army knives, spare change. Why not shoelaces? Because of human folly, that's all. We just don't have our priorities right. Just consider this: there's not much point in having an extra umbrella if one of your shoes falls off while you are walking in the rain. There's not much point in carrying extra money if your laces break and the stores are closed. Many people don't even keep extra shoelaces at home — if you can believe that.

After the discomfort and the confusion comes, eventually, that moment when new laces must be put in. It is that moment that concerns us here because it is a moment when you know the greatest peace you will ever know. A loose shoe is like having no face. A loose shoe is like finding out that your mother was promiscuous nine months before you were born. A loose shoe is like finding out that your Ph.D. was an April Fools' joke. A loose shoe is like becoming the head of an English Department.

When the new laces are available and you take off your shoe, thread the lace through the bottom two eyelets, pull the ends even and thread them to the top, your mind is at peace. When the laces are in and you put the shoe back on and pull the laces tight and tie them snugly, you feel confidence and exuberance. The firm grip of the shoe on your foot makes you feel like running out and leaping through the dandelions. You feel like making love to any barefoot woman you might find. You feel like forgiving your father and mother for having given you life. You feel like reading a fairy tale to your children. You feel like whistling the "Hallelujah Chorus" from *The Messiah*. You can strut out and do all these things because power has been restored to your conscience, your mind and your imagination. Not to mention your vision.

A broken shoelace is thus a sign of imminent greatness. While putting new laces in his shoes, Homer thought of Odysseus. While threading in new laces, Aristotle thought of the *Metaphysics*. While tying firmly his new laces, Ovid thought of *The Metamorphoses*. When John the Baptist put new laces into Christ's shoes, Christ realized that he was the son of God. While putting new laces in their shoes, Dante conceived the *Paradise*, Shakespeare imagined Sir Andrew Aguecheek, Milton understood *Paradise Regained*, Blake thought of "Jerusalem" and William Carlos Williams thought of *Paterson*. While imagining a pair of shoes and imagining that he was putting new laces in them, Alfred Jarry conceived Père Ubu. Just yesterday, I myself put new laces into my shoes and I conceived this essay.

A broken shoelace is a sign from God that you are about to face your best self. It is a blessing hidden in discomfort. It is a sign that God cares and that he wishes you to reassert the goodness, the imagination and nobility that are within you. When a lace wears out and snaps while you are running to get your income tax in on time, it is an intimation that God cares about your priorities. If a lace breaks while you are writing a story, it is a sign that it will be published. If a lace breaks while you are kneeling and praying, it is a sign that your prayers will be answered. It is a sign that your soul will be restored and order will return into your universe. A broken shoelace and a flopping shoe are a heavenly voice telling you to be ready.

I have a confession to make. I present myself to this world as Peter Solomon Seiltanzer. I'm sometimes called "Skyblue" or, at certain moments, "Skyblue the Badass." I am an Assistant Professor of English at the University of Cincinnati. I have never published a thing, so I will probably retire at that rank. No one seems interested in my special study of "Pastoral Dichotomies and Ambivalences in Small Farm Apprehensions." I live in a one-room apartment on Riddle Road in Cincinnati, Ohio. My only living relative is Ben Kitzler, who is the town drunk in Newton, Kansas.

Many scholars deal with the problem of "appearance versus reality." My appearance is what I have just said. My reality is otherwise. And that is my confession. You see, I'm really not what I seem to be. Actually, I am a shepherd. Because of technological progress, I can no longer be what I really am. I was born to be a shepherd, I was trained to be a shepherd and I still want to be what I was destined to be. I want to sit on the ground, watch my flocks by night and wait for the glory of the Lord to come upon me. I want to see all that and go out to a stable and see what's there.

Now there ain't no pastures. And because there ain't no pastures there ain't no sheep. And because there ain't no sheep, there ain't no shepherds. And because there ain't no shepherds there's no one out there waiting for the Messiah to come. And because no one's waiting, He won't come. Someone has to sit and wait. No one's waiting and we're all lost.

I've always refused to think that I am lost. That's why some people thought that I had a stiff right leg. There was nothing wrong with my leg. My leg seemed stiff because I carried a fold-up shepherd's crook in my right pantleg. The crook was in three pieces and folded out into a complete crook. I carried it there in case I happened to pass a pasture with sheep in it. When that happened, I stopped my car, got out, unfolded the crook, crawled through the fence and the "no trespassing" signs and stood with the sheep until fired upon. When the sheep scattered and went astray, I ran back to my car, refolded the crook and wondered if the Messiah had anything to do with it.

The state of Ohio has an official "state shepherd." I once applied for the job. That meant I had to have an interview with James Rhodes, the governor. I made an appointment and walked into his office. He said, "I see you have a gimpy leg." "Well, governor," I said, "there's nothing wrong with my leg. It's my crook." "Your crook?" he said. "That's right," I said. He said, "Let's see it," so I unzipped my fly and pulled out the curved top. "My God," he said, "I've never seen one like that before." As I pulled out more of the shaft, he began bleating and slobbering. When I pulled it all out and unfolded it, he cried out, as he fainted away, "You got the job."

Now, on weekends, I drive the highways and byways of Ohio, looking for pastures with sheep in them. The "no trespassing" signs have been outlawed by the state legislature. Buckshot may not be used in pastures. The taxpayers of Ohio have given me a new aluminum crook that is in one piece. I have a rack on top of my blue VW and I can strap my crook to it. The Messiah has been given a visa to the state. Two days a week I wait. My sheep know my voice and I know them. They wait at the fences for my skyblue arrival.

As I sit on the hillsides, keeping watch, the sheep lie down beside me. They chew their cuds and nuzzle my right leg. As the midnight hour comes upon us, I confess to them that I have a Ph.D., that I teach at a university, that I live in a one-room apartment in a city, that I come to them only on weekends and that I am ashamed of the whole world.

DAMON KRUKOWSKI

• • •

THE INTELLECTUAL LIFE

One word presents itself before others: simplify. You have
a difficult voyage; you must lie down; is there a law
to govern the necessary estrangement, pushing through the crowd,
cutting of teeth — is there a road away from the village,
and toward the problem at hand? One can always reveal *the soul;*
fingers draw the curtain apart; a card game is in progress;
but one mustn't hitch dissimilar animals, one needn't solve
the wrong problems. The game, though visible, is nonetheless
an argument for solitude. Cooperate with your peers; cultivate
necessary relations; yet conserve your fair share of necessary action.
Maintain above all an interior silence. Reduce your rate
of expenditure. Conserve the flux of thought, chattering mind.

"It is not necessary to believe," writes Mme. de B. in her journal,
"that the best and sole use of time is calm, sustained, and ordered.
Agitation is a useful state of mind; corresponding as it does
to our actual state of being. One mustn't think that work is more
than a supplement of possibilities to the achievement of one's being."

THE MINOR POETS

One knows nothing of their life. The sea
has taken all. I have no boat, and no
companions. Only one thing is left: *my love
for you.*

One follows hunches. One debates the established
rules. In effect, one completes — in this latter
half of a divided century — an anthology of ten volumes
of three hundred pages each, all in small type.

O Penelope, it's only chance that brought you unlucky
Ulysses; looking at your careful writing on this package
I feel the weight of my own torments.
You accuse me of indolence. I only want to listen
to your account of suffering.

ELKE ERB

•.•

DIARY ENTRY, JANUARY SEVEN

Visited the jumping Jack, who moves all by himself, and an expecting mother. A fly kept hitting the lamp, buzzing so loudly we could hardly hear what we were saying. There ought to be a Chinese character to put a seal on such adverse conditions and lock them in the bookcase once and for all.

Walls, if you let them, drift down the mountain side and out over the sea. My mountains in Berlin-Mitte are called: stomach ache, belly ache, rotten sleep, damage done.

My new apartment must have dropped out of a capitalist's pants pocket in the 'nineties. This man, of whom I know nothing else, beheaded an egg every morning, and this man's better half wore for jewelry cast iron earrings from the royal Prussian foundry.

To keep ferrets as an environment, why not? They would run back and forth on the bare floor, a good idea, albinos with white fur, they'd look up with inflamed eyes. Even my afternoons would then appear white with small pinkish eyes and take on shape. We'd just have to store everything a couple of feet off the floor to avoid damage.

BICKERING

While you would find my two sisters bickering almost whenever you looked, I, the oldest by two years, was "quiet" and "reasonable." They drew sparks from each other, and their energy exploded the more fiercely because our environment was too busy rebuilding cities and correcting the past to pay attention to such appeals of childish and immature passion. But even I, docile pupil of a narrowly rational and logical system of education, tried, brooding — while the two of them, rolled into one ball of contention, brushed past me — to fight the stony dreariness, to mine with fuses and dynamite the colossal rock of inevitability before me. Surely it must open, nay change into a magic garden of fulfilment, once I thought everything through and found the pass word. At bottom, so I remained convinced, everything is simple and in harmony with us. So what was the big difference between me and my sisters? Doesn't it amount to the same thing whether you fight all the time or hang on to one conviction with all your might? Isn't either one absolutely childish? Not a difference of character or even temperament. Noisy or quiet! Don't we know how loud silence can be? But with their squabbles, children, even without meanness, yank at all the roots they vie to sink into their real estate in the world — a process of development with tests and failures, probations and growth, which is by no means sure to encourage the most desirable and happy traits. Today I hear those childhood squabbles as — unmistakable! — uninterrupted sobbing.

WELL, IS IT GOING TO BUDGE, THE BEAST?

I mounted, to escape the empty blackness, the inevitable misery of rain puddles at night, and the still gloomier (on top of all the gloom, still gloomier) rumors of the center, I mounted, a nephew on the shoulders of an uncle unwilling to let the nephew inherit, the humped shoulders of one of the two ill-tempered, elephantine cows — with heads like elks?! — pressed with the two white beams of my legs and my labia till heat rose from humped ill temper, and so got off rather easy, off the siding with hissing, elbow-pumping, old-timer locomotives, in one of those nights when you look at a sky finite like torture in every inch of pain, lined with dark velvet, with tiny pointed upholstery nails for stars.

THIS AND THAT

This village clings to rock like a swallow's nest to the eaves. Its products are . . . and the fine-spun thread of fate.

That village lies at the tip of the tongue of a peninsula by the sea. It supplies fishery products, peat, milk, meat, eggs and . . .

Another village in the plains of the hinterland yields mainly grain, potatoes, carrots, dairy products, hops, vegetables.

Yet another one, in Georgia, tea.

I don't want to make pronouncements about destiny, except: they produce, work, harvest, exchange.

I was struck by the sight, as I went down to the village, of a woman sitting in the yard, in the sun, on Sunday afternoon, by a little table, over a piece of cloth she was embroidering, while all around roofs, windows, trees and the gently rising green slopes of the village looked down on her who, deeply intent on her embroidery, had no eyes for the road, me, us, things, sheds, the chicken coop, no eyes for weeds, the fence, the road, the nearby village pond down the road.

One free hour, and there she sits and embroiders.

BANAT MUSEUM

Two pieces of ornamental stone, of identical size, from the collection BASRELIEFURI FRAGMENTARE DIN MARMORA / TIBISCUM. One with two human feet (damaged), the other with a dog's foot beside two human feet with strikingly long toes next to a hoof (?), all on the bottom shelf of a glass case. There is also a single human arm with a hand (damaged) closed over something that has been lost . . .

THE STOVE PROBLEM

We have a stove in the big hall all right, but can't get it warm. The
parquet freezes over, and since we don't want to freeze also, we
skate, around and around. Eyed from the ceiling by a hundred
indifferent icicles, we skate through the mist rising from the far
corners of the hall and think we can see bushes, nature in
hibernation. The stove is no good. No matter how many logs
and how much coal we throw in, it gives out only a tenth of the
heat it's supposed to. Once, years ago, our poor father with his
narrow shoulders, and the rest of us, spent weeks setting up a
series of stoves at a distance of 1.20 meters each between them, a
whole chain of stoves lining the hall. But we were wrong to think
the heat would add up. Each stove gave a tenth, and all in all it
remained a tenth: the stoves did not communicate. In a case
where all are insufficient it is sufficient for one to be insufficient.
So, in order not to endanger the clarity of the situation, we took
all the other stoves out again. And so we skate on, round and
round. And life too goes round and round in a circle, which, I
have to admit, the stove problem, even though insoluble,
touches and — almost — intersects.

translated from the German by Rosmarie Waldrop

MARCEL COHEN

•   •   •

from: *THE PEACOCK EMPEROR MOTH*

The water came up to his waist. He plunged in, took twenty or so strokes out and then turned around to look at the beach with its vacationers. Thousands of voices rang like notes held on bass strings under an unleashing, and against the extreme metallic stridence, of scattered flutes. The sea was warm and clear: he was able to see, in the transparence, the shadow of his body lighten on the sandy bottom as he drew away from it. And the thought came to him, so limpid, too, and so blunt that he had nothing to oppose it: his life seemed like the effort of a swimmer unable to move, struggling, through imperceptible movements, to keep his body from covering up his shadow.

The director of a museum of natural history admits to anxiety in the face of the rapid mutations of certain animal species. Forced to emigrate and adapt, many increase in anarchic ways. Attracted by garbage disposal dumps, dozens of thousands of silver seagull couples and laughing sea-mews prosper now on the outskirts of big cities: some airports are no longer safe. Curtailing their migrations, starlings swoop by the millions down upon the harvests. Bred for their fur, muskrats and coypou escaped from cages mine the dikes and banks of the rivers. The mole, the marten and the fox settle down in the heart of cities, eluding predators and traps. The cricket elects to reside in the Paris Metro, the scorpion between the stones of historical monuments. Singing till quite recently only at twilight, the inoffensive blackbird itself can now be heard all night long, perfectly accustomed to city lights.

Revolt in an institution for paraplegics: some centimeters too high through an architectural error, the windows don't allow the sea close by to be seen from gurneys and wheelchairs.

A lone in his room, a man wonders night after night about the sounds filtering through the partition: music in the next apartment, very muffled, but recognizable once he puts his ear to the wall, slight squeaks on the parquet floor, brief outbursts of voices. Some evenings, fascinated by the distance as much as by the very proximity he bangs listlessly on the wall with the stone of his signet-ring. The message then comes in return: three short, clear, raps, impossible to interpret in the great silence.

E very evening, returning from his forest walk, a man goes out of his way to be at this spectacle which attracts as much as it disconcerts him: the two daughters of the forest-ranger at their lessons, seated on the stoop, books on their laps; the kitchen window open, where the mother bustles about in the encroaching dusk; a doll abandoned at the foot of a tree; the ranger's bike set against a euonymus hedge; the man, finally, whom the scraping of some tool locates in the kitchen garden. The sun is on the mountain tops. In a few minutes, the dog is sure to pull on his leash, barking.

The walker knows he will find nowhere else as finely-woven a nest of appearances. However, there isn't anything yet, to his eyes, that begins to look like proof. He feels both richer and, by that infirmity which always reverses signs, robbed of a mirage.

P retending to be very sensitive to light, a young woman never takes off her outsize sunglasses in which her admirers are annoyed at seeing only their own smiles. Measured unwittingly, confronted by their own caricature when they look for some encouragement (but not giving up hope of overcoming the distance at which they think they're being kept playfully), how could they help feeling particularly gauche?

Yet the young woman can make out only blurry figures stirring about. Three-quarters blind from an accident, and using all her coquetry not to let it be seen, she feels herself exposed defenceless to their eyes.

He'd never dreamt of killing himself before, and the idea remained almost completely alien to him. Alone on his balcony, however, in his moments of utter boredom, wondering about his constant temptation to jump anyhow, he found, as answer, only a really insane curiosity: to appraise exactly what infinitesimal, but very real, part chance might play in the virtual certainty of his dying in the act.

A man is putting together his curriculum vitae when he's swept by an extreme lassitude. He takes off his glasses, leans against the back of his armchair, pivots it towards the window and loses himself in what's going on in the street. He should have every reason to be proud of his life's balance-sheet: from distortion to distortion he wonders only if his biography reflects him yet.

After five years in prison a man is about to get out. He had insisted that his wife stop coming to see him at visiting times nor write to him either. This way she would perhaps be freer to forget him.

He writes a note to her now, indicating the day and hour he is to be set free. No need for her, he explains, to come pick him up, much less to give any account of the free time she hadn't sought. With their house being visible from the railway tracks, it would be enough if she just hang a cloth from one of the windows if she cares to have him come by. Otherwise he won't get off the train and simply continue on his way.

An invalid studying himself day after day in his mirror and, he believes, without kidding himself. He keeps an eye on his weight, watches for the slightest changes in his body. He knows his illness is at a standstill, is undoubtedly even in remission.

What he reads on the faces of his kin, whatever he catches from their conversations and marks in their countless attentions, tends however to persuade him, a little more each day, of the opposite.

A painter sitting at the bedside where his father lies dead and trying, reverently, to fix one last time his features in a drawing. While he works, he keeps coming up against John Berger's statement in similar circumstances: nothing differentiates what he sets down on the paper from what he would draw were his father only asleep. In front of the finished drawing, however, who would not make the distinction?

A man wakes up in the middle of the night. His wife is no longer beside him, but he hears her moving about in the next room.

He gets up to join her and, attracted by the light directly striking the curtains in their bedroom, makes a detour towards the window: from the other side of the street, because of the darkness, the image of his companion is reflected in the bakery window.

The man looks on, incapable now of detaching himself from the image, as if the distance and the intrusion could finally reveal what their proximity has always concealed.

An insomniac decides to walk at random in the Paris streets. He discovers, week after week, the rapture of wresting from night long hours of consciousness, of living, in short, by intruding.

Soon, however, he wonders if he hasn't merely tilted into the imaginary, if he isn't already a pure figment fearing the light of day.

An entomologist is breaking his back to raise in a laboratory lepidopterae on the road to extinction. Because the females only rarely lay eggs in captivity, the battle is almost in vain, he knows, for the majority of the diurnal species decimated by pesticides. Some moths, on the other hand, mate when caged and, when set free, can detect a single flower ten kilometers off. That's why, he is convinced, the Peacock Emperor Moth, some thirty million years old, will almost alone outlive the last diurnal butterfly.

translated from the French by Cid Corman

CLAUDE ROYET-JOURNOUD

• ••

from: *I. E.*

1   behind the image
    there is no further recourse
    the inertia of things empties out emotion

    —

    one last time
    he accompanies the noise

    the space around

2   but the palm is visible

    you are smack in the dark
    beyond bewilderment

    — a room to which this word has come —

    —

    no reason
    to go there
    I see nothing but a wall

3   I can no longer talk to you
     legs carry the alphabet
     fall for space

—

it's in the interior that —

time turned back
on his lips
without remembering the spot

4   "an accident struck this word"
     a word he was just looking for
     there where nothing moves

—

don't hit

outside
you would no longer know

"and every time he would describe a circle
around the thing"

5   your hand draws back from the motive
to grasp an elbow, a shoulder
unknowing it crosses
it is what ceases to be

the beast dies in a crease of the page
it offers a moment of enjoyment

conversation picks up again

—

here an incoherent blue overhangs
the square

6   some *invisible vowels*

like thought
the resemblance
is at syllable's edge

eye pursues its prey
shelters behind another phrase

where to find the precise strength

darkness counts down
the hand announces its failure

no alignment
a nerve discerns daylight

translated from the French by Keith Waldrop

PAUL AUSTER

•   •   •

"IT REMINDS ME OF SOMETHING THAT ONCE HAPPENED TO MY MOTHER . . ."

In 1974, I was invited by Anthony Rudolf to contribute an article to the London magazine, *European Judaism*, for an issue celebrating Charles Reznikoff's eightieth birthday. I had been living in France for the past four years, and the little piece I sent in on Reznikoff's work was the first thing I wrote after coming back to America. It seemed like a fitting way to mark my return.

I moved into an apartment on Riverside Drive in late summer. After finishing the article, I discovered that Reznikoff lived very near by — on West End Avenue — and sent him a copy of the manuscript, along with a letter asking him if it would be possible for us to meet. Several weeks went by without a response.

On a Sunday in early October I was to be married. The ceremony was scheduled to take place in the apartment at around noon. At eleven o'clock, just moments before the guests were to arrive, the telephone rang and an unfamiliar voice asked to speak to me. "This is Charles Reznikoff," the voice said, in a sing-song tone, looping ironically and with evident good humor. I was, of course, pleased and flattered by the call, but I explained that it would be impossible for me to talk just now. I was about to be married, and I was in no condition to form a coherent sentence. Reznikoff was highly amused by this and burst out laughing. "I never called a man on his wedding day before!" he said. "Mazel tov, mazel tov!" We arranged to meet the following week at his apartment. Then I hung up the phone and marched off to the altar.

Reznikoff's apartment was on the twenty-second floor of a large building complex, with a broad, uncluttered view of the Hudson and sunlight pouring through the windows. I arrived in the middle of the day, and with a somewhat stale crumb cake set before me and numerous cups of coffee to drink, I wound up staying three or four hours. The visit made such an impression on me that even now, almost a decade later, it is entirely present inside of me.

I have met some good story-tellers in my life, but Reznikoff was the champion. Some of his stories that day went on for thirty or forty minutes, and no matter how far he seemed to drift from the point he was supposedly trying to make, he was in complete control. He had the patience that is necessary to the telling of a good story — and the ability to savor the least detail that cropped up along the way. What at first seemed to be an endless series of digressions, a kind of aimless wandering, turned out to be the elaborate and systematic construction of a circle. For example: why did you come back to New York after living in Hollywood? There followed a myriad of little incidents: meeting the brother of a certain man on a park bench, the color of someone's eyes, an economic crisis in some country. Fifteen minutes later, just when I was beginning to feel hopelessly lost — and convinced that Reznikoff was lost, too — he would begin a slow return to his starting point. Then, with great clarity, and conviction, he would announce: "So that's why I left Hollywood." In retrospect, it all made perfect sense.

I heard stories about his childhood, his aborted career in journalism, his law studies, his work for his parents as a jobber of hats and how he would write poems on a bench at Macy's while waiting his turn to show the store buyer his samples. There were also stories about his walks — in particular, his journey from New York to Cape Cod (on foot!), which he undertook when he was well past sixty. The important thing, he explained, was not to walk too fast. Only by forcing himself to keep the pace of less than two miles per hour could he be sure to see everything he wanted to see.

On my visit that day, I brought along for him a copy of my first book of poems, *Unearth*, which had just been published. This evoked a story from Reznikoff that strikes me as significant, especially in the light of the terrible neglect his work suffered for so many years. His first book, he told me, had been published in 1918 by Samuel Roth (who would later become famous for pirating *Ulysses* and his role in the 1933 court case over Joyce's book). The leading American poet of the day was Edwin Arlington Robinson, and Reznikoff had sent him a copy of the book, hoping for some sign of encouragement from the great man. One afternoon Reznikoff was visiting Roth in his bookstore, and Robinson walked in. Roth went over to greet him, and Reznikoff, standing in the back corner of the shop, witnessed the following scene. Roth proudly gestured to the copies of Reznikoff's book that were on display and asked Robinson if he had read the work of this fine young poet. "Yeah, I read the book," said Robinson in a gruff, hostile voice, "and I thought it was garbage."

"And so," said Reznikoff to me in 1974, "I never got to meet Edwin Arlington Robinson."

It was not until I was putting on my coat and getting ready to leave that Reznikoff said anything about the piece I had sent him. It had been composed in an extremely dense and cryptic style, wrestling with issues that Reznikoff himself had probably never consciously thought about, and I had no idea what his reaction would be. His silence about it during our long conversation led me to suspect that he had not liked it.

"About your article," he said, almost off-handedly. "It reminds me of something that once happened to my mother. A stranger walked up to her on the street one day and very kindly and graciously complimented her on her beautiful hair. Now you must understand that my mother had never prided herself on her hair and did not consider it to be one of her better features. But, on the strength of that stranger's remark, she spent most of the day in front of her mirror, preening and primping and admiring her hair. That's exactly what your article did to me. I stood in front of the mirror for the whole afternoon and admired myself."

Several weeks later, I received a letter from Reznikoff about my book. It was filled with praise, and the numerous quotations from the poems convinced me that he was in earnest — that he had actually sat down and read the book. Nothing could have meant more to me.

A few years after Reznikoff's death, a letter came to me from La Jolla, written by a friend who works in the American Poetry Archive at the University of California library — where Reznikoff's papers had recently been sold. In going through the material, my friend told me, he had come across Reznikoff's copy of *Unearth*. Astonishingly, the book was filled with numerous small notations in the margins, as well as stress marks that Reznikoff had made throughout the poem in an effort to scan them correctly and understand their rhythms. Helpless to do or say anything, I thanked him from the other side of the grave.

Wherever Edwin Arlington Robinson might be now, one can be sure that his accommodations aren't half as good as Charles Reznikoff's.

LISA JARNOT

•• •

DIARY OF A ROUGH TRADE ANGEL

chapter one

and then help me because and then and help and then i said i won you
said i said i won and we were in a car and countries are toppling i said
and style and then and help i said are toppling my style and dictate then
and help and then i said i won you said and help and then and car i said
and car i said and help i said and then i said a car i said and we were in
a car and countries are toppling i said are next to my summer address
and then i said is next to my style i said are raspberries said and summer
addressed and ferris wheel wrench and then

and then help me because and then cut me. and help and then i won i
said in a car and countries are toppling. i say i love you/dog me. i say
hurt me mr. sir and my summer address is next to the raspberries in the
ferris wheel wrench.

chapter two

and hear me the modern received i and letters today i and landlords but
better the fox holes and leave i across i receive i the landlords and letters
across all the countries are toppling but won i of spelled wrong the
wrong i and down i the one i and i i but war torn and hurt i but spelled
wrong and down i and called i but lame i and hurt i was wheel i and
paged me the tight i my hurt i and then i

take twenty pounds of heavy weights and hear me modern that i
received today a mail of letters better than that. tell of countries all across

the country spelled wrong, of landlords all across the country spelled wrong down one fox hole and out the next. page me once and then he said my name and called but he was

chapter three

not like you my rabbit master.

not like you my rabbit master.

chapter four

no loves i was not aware at the time of the time at the place where they come like you the thieves and landlords are come at the spelled wrong aware of at time that the sober are time and the power of time and that no loves aware of the time of the master was joking at sweetness and then said to like

i like it i said when you say that in the back of the bar next to lewis.

when, in the back of the bar (next to lewis) you say that i like it.

when, having said that you say that, i say that you said that i like it (in the back of the bar next to lewis).

when they come again, the thieves and the landlords, no loves, i was not aware at the time of the power of time and i never saw so sober sweetness, i was only joking when i said i like it when you say that in the back of the bar next to lewis.

chapter five

ever i'd stand to know your walk and clever i'd stand to watch
your drink and ever i'd fall to run your hands across my
crossed i'd never and then i'd long to take your ledge

that you were tying around my neck and

ever i'd take to clever return to find you ever in each at not a good idea
that down by the river runs your hands some ever across my cross like
limbs of the crossed i'd take to

time

me up and run your home across my hands some then that this is not a
good idea to watch and step and dark

epilogue

if ever there was a mistake it was at the verge of this link called the cuffed
and the clever

ever to clever the cuff at the hedge,

(what i mean pierre is ever. stop. to stand for the cuff in the hedge. stop.
ever to clever. stop. what i mean. stop. pierre. stop me. stop. and then
some i long for to run at the river. so stopped at the bridge. stop. and ever
the clever. stop. ever to clever to me at to time me to up to the watch step
and dark. stop. step at the verge of and walk at the watch step and dark
at the clever at ever the edge. stop. what at the hand of. stop. at the watch
step. stop. and verge of the dark. stop at the clever and ever to. stop.
crossed at the clever and cuffed with an ever and then some. to stop.)

JESSICA LOWENTHAL

•*•

HOVERING

1

Wings blur, a bird hovers

in one place. Imagine *beginning*
as fixed like that, a moment

of potential flight, a moment defined
in the delicate balance

of *lift*

2

In the beginning was the bird and the bird was with god and the
bird was god. He was in the beginning *with* god. All things were
made through him, and without him nothing was made that was
made

Nothing was made that was made. All bird in beginning and
nothing was made. In the beginning was nothing and nothing
was made. He was not made, bird was not made, nothing was
made

He was not made, *all* birds unmade. Bird in beginning, all birds
unmade. He did it un-bird, the birdless beginning. He did it all
through him and nothing was made

3

In space, in the rapid flutter of its wings.

In moments before and after flight, in the hovering of potential.

The fluttering of wings has no part in it. A body

has no correspondence with flight. A body hovers

to think of it. The fluttering of wings notwithstanding.

Perhaps there are bodies in correspondence

4

if there are bodies at all.
Imagine beginning as fixed like *that*.
A body hovers and nothing is made

MARK McMORRIS

• • •

GEOMETRY OF THE FIGURE

I.

Day plain and un-cluttered
with voices, a night thick with scent
of bodies given up to the grass
black bodies in a compass
the center and exits of the house
opening to admit them

II.

Entangled in circles of light
as ropes of the wheel, an old horse
given up to spheres of the heart
night-long in the pound
turning the wheel of their breath

III.

Circles punctured by cones
day pricked through with stars
all the yard long in his labor
the old horse lucid with his sweat
moving the wheel of their talk

IV.

The yard circles in this space
day and night the fire, a half-light
to cheat the shadows of their milk
one stillness for both, one body
bodies in the deep air of January
that enters and stills, and holds them

V.

And in the stillness only
the sphere and balancing apples
moving with premonitions of light
the fanfare of angels, bewildered
at the oscillation of waters
and the bird of summer, flown

VI.

The seed of perishing holds
the cavity of the sphere
and around it lies day, spacious
to the edge of the land-mass
mesmeric, the breaths of stillness
within the seed, and the sphere

VII.

The long-lived affairs of light
the budding impression of branches
eager to come close to the fullness
a rippling on the sheets, and water,
fire and light of the vineyard

VIII.

A stillness forms where they talk
at the farthest point which is still
spinning and at rest, at peace —
harbingers of the night to come
a last beginning of the day-song

JACQUELINE RISSET

● ● ●

VOICE

world put back on its
wheels
if at night
you have

---

ringing
dark surrounding
not your voice :
picking up :
no one
yet

---

not your very breath
but
your call
it was
when I
hang up you

---

touch and the world
is touched
slips
oiled
this empty
sign
you give
then

---

time
exists
you are —
which image

or pain
do you read
have you read?
but this here

---

without importance
since you
are
saying
by this act
"I
am"
and I —
this

---

we
then —
again —
you saw I saw
you
without your voice
yet saying —
not your voice

---

my voice
without answer
but
at present
you living

---

under the same ones
into the same —
then I —
live ?

translated from the French by Jennifer Moxley

ALAIN VEINSTEIN

• •   •

from: *EVEN A CHILD*

FROM FAR

From far, with the child,
not with my words.

Enclosed there, like other times,
with no word, without change.

No step taken, like before,
and this is only part of the day.

———

Nobody at the beginning.
This room. The silence, Impossible
to know if the day dawned.
I look for words of a lost sentence
a line from the time when I lived
from my work . . .

———

Much later, I don't know which day,
not a word in return, the silence,
a hand's weight
as never love . . .
My child (who can say that?)
it's possible, so it is possible —
even a child
in this room where we grimace
because of the sun.

———

"Faded from us
from the start . . ."

"I'd gladly spill my
blood to put an end
to this begging . . ."

Toward the absence of support
return to ground, outstretched.

translated from the French by Robert Kocik

ILMA RAKUSA

•   ••

ROSA AGHIOS or THE JOURNEY

My third attempt at an interpretation failed as well. It was not a teenage school girl with burning cheeks and indivisible desire who sat opposite me, but a Rosa from Friaul, half girl, half woman, servant in a great house. She stared out at the rugged landscape, murmuring "Ajax" from time to time and twiddling her thumbs. I thought she was in love or a little confused, but she gave more details. Home, yes, where there was a stone house and a garden of stinging nettles. There she would creep up on the rarest birds, would bury her arms in warm hay. There she would abandon herself to a hundred different thoughts, reading amongst the cabbage leaves. None of this concentrated light, she summed up, the sky is matt and my father limps.

Accident at work?

Feeding deer.

With these words her enthusiasm flagged. I saw Rosa cross an abandoned street with a civilian, the rows of firs, of pears and apples had not yet passed by while she accused herself of having hats instead of relatives.

Ajax.

Sorry?

Oh, that doesn't belong here. The rosy-cheeked deer roam particularly close to the house.

With equal aimlessness I relinquished myself to my thoughts. Here, Rosa, speckled like a rainbow trout, there a Doctor of Political Economy, between them a circle of knitting virgins — I pushed against the direction of travel, against all evidence, into my future behind me. Let's call it Trieste. Let's assume it's fed by a regular breaking of surf. Henchmen aren't henchmen, but gentleness and determination are also gone. And as I beg indulgence, the cape withdraws, exposing ever more compact views. Something like that.

I thought of Rosa again. Rivers that flow against the current are her favourite, the coast wind damages the ears and at the edge of any feasting you'll find Mr Excessive.

I nodded. How old could Rosa be, that she dragged Time along like a piece of string? After all, she was moving in the direction of travel and Friaul was where it was.

Rosa Aghios. *The tall, young, blonde woman with the sweet figure, only her hands showing the marks of hard work.* And Aghios shouted: *But why must my daughter lie beneath me like that? I don't want her. It's not my fault.* Deer feeding and a lemon-yellow book, only I didn't like to ask her. Rosa dozed with her thumbs in motion, as though she were grinding river sand.

In the dream, Mr Aghios's rotting face had lain against a vehicle. Beneath him endless space, above, the same. At Görz his dream began to relax. He let his head sink onto the upholstery, climbed into his own childhood and forgot the signorina. Instead he saw an empty field, a farmhouse and smoky light. He suffered no pangs of conscience, for he travelled towards his solitude. With that he also buried the legend of the double journey.

Rosa was sleeping. Or was she? In different lights her hands flickered up, her lap became a white apron and I felt I could make out Ajax, surrounded by the smell of herbs and cold. Time drives the past before it like jetsam, all silence is chatter, except your own name. Rosa Aghios. *Do you want me with you?* Mr Aghios pressed himself even more firmly against his vehicle so as to remain unseen. He travelled in a spaceship, in a gondola, in a barque, in the Görz-Trieste freight train. *I want my son not to stay alone.* After this opening Rosa asked: *And what should you do with your lack of freedom, if all around there is only enslavement?*

Rosa, Rosa. She dreamed animal dreams while the river, swollen with melt water frightened me from beyond the train window. The ice-grey water ran down to the valley floor. Constantly breaking its own shadow pattern and roughening the bank. Compared to that my surf broke gently.

Who's stumbling?

The horse, I whispered startled, as though I had to save Rosa's sleep. With sloping ribs.

She blinked. The nag, that's not good.

So things weren't looking too good in Friaul. I was just going to ask her about the abandoned street, about the civilian and the stillness entwined in green, but her gaze was caught by the swirling river.

Quite an epic, I said, to my own surprise.

Whatever, she replied calmly. The poor, poor horses. What I don't understand, is this confusion on earth and beyond.

Now was my moment to mention Mr Aghios's dream-spaceship, with which he had intended to escape this very confusion — there, Rosa, between Görz and Trieste —, instead I declared carelessly that it was a matter of altering boundaries.

And that's supposed to give direction?

Direction, yes.

Sideways or upwards?

Whichever you want.

It was hard to say whether Rosa was thinking of her master or of the edges of her valley. Her thumbs moved slowly, as though each movement checked off one more possibility.

Sideways, she decided, because I often feel hemmed in. Whole cliffs cave in and there's no escape.

The valley: the garden full of nettles, the snuffling pigs, barbed fences, deer feeding in the pine forests, further up rocky, then snowy peaks, oh yes, and the nags in their shafts along the abandoned street.

Rosa Aghios wore patent leather shoes. In the unpaved valley she was greeted and parted from simply. It happened so quickly that she couldn't remember ever having arrived. So was she dreaming upright, with Time undecided?

They dropped me. First misjudged, then pushed to the fore, then dropped. If you're going to dance to a stranger's tune, they said, then you can't expect to warm yourself in the snows of home.

Tired moss, I said. An epic in moss form.

I don't fiddle about now, I follow my chosen path.

Rosa had herself under control. What united us was our past future in Julian-Venice or wherever. I too had been dropped from the valley anti-patent-leather-shoe-club. Since then I've felt like talking about the sun.

A simple departure isn't worth discussing, she said.

And what do you do if two fatherlands lay claim?

As though caught red-handed she mumbled "Ajax" and that change had changed.

You're withholding your lover or the unknown soldier.

Rosa wasn't listening. Ajax was driving her in another direction and I realised it was too late for Mr Aghios. She had lured him into the trap of monogamy and absinthe.

Rosa with the emotional thumbs. Whispering, she vouched for something. And just as I wanted to ask her about her motherland, she complained that she felt hemmed in by my nervous feet.

Two roe deer.

Who for?

That would need considering.

I didn't have an Ajax, not even a home town that I could have suppressed. Who for then?

Are you trying to sit up again?

With my left leg, the right one wants to do something different.

And your self-esteem?

I forgave her the nosy question. There were rare days when I had some. On a windy February morning when nobody wanted anything from me, I carried my head higher. Then it seemed possible to alter everything, to keep animals with Egyptian confidence. And a canary whistled in the square of my dreams.

Inside herself she could only hear voices saying no, although she still kept on working towards the edges, towards these eastern borders, towards this Friaul nonsense. Oh yes, I am not called Hortense and my parents are not advantaged! Her voice cracked. Welcome and it's all over!

It was only now that I noticed that her eyes were changing colour and that our union was already advanced. From the heights of his journey, Mr Aghios had recognised the domestic pet in man, Rosa extinguished herself more and more, that made her strong. One day there she would be with a new name, on the plains.

I forgot the imagined rifts and my reasons for walking into the sea. Be forgotten as quickly as possible, red collar turned up and better uphill than downhill.

I only mean that we need a more powerful proposal.

Just don't reveal any meeting-places!

That's one of my ground rules.

Rosa's eyes shone.

There are too many cupboards in the house and the street has gone to pot.

Don't worry.

The dust causes nausea and coughing.

Whatever.

I didn't want to hear any more about the missing paddocks, after all you don't have to abandon yourself to a village where the thatch is loose.

Rosa Aghios twiddled her thumbs gratefully. Her speckled face showed the first hint of a smile.

I'll tell Rosalie.

Good.

And I showed her the *flurry of light.*

translated from the German by Solveig Emerson

SIANNE NGAI

•   •   •

from: *DISCREDIT*

How any face looks at itself
in the next room, or what is in the mind before the onset of pictures.
Which is possibly the mind, asking: is it disguise enough just to be here?
Everyone has an emergency voice.

A book you read
describes "a foolish period of history"

as if one could be moved by the efforts of either army
or multiple ways of meaning it
faster.

The yardstick growing out of your body tells you its growth has been
    stunted.

—

Telephone pole which has lost its height — how else do you know
what you've done?
A difference between a protest and a greeting which
might stop you dead, on the edge of the pavement. Either way.
It might make sense

to say ordinary things—
"You make my face as dead as you are." In the cancellation of metaphor
the feet stand in inches.
They are.

—

For a mirror to find the mirror the face needs to disappear, as when
    there is a choice
to explain or say nothing, to trust or be suspicious.
Buzz and cloud
in their respective suffocations.

& nearness has to be more
than "I've noticed things have happened
more 'recently' than before."

Big coat demanding
a citizen and not because of the weather involved.
There are people for this and people for that

but when rumors fail to exaggerate, who doesn't feel the left sleeve
    drag?

KEITH WALDROP

• • •

POET

The wind dying, I find a city deserted, except for crowds of people moving and standing.

Those standing resemble stories, like stones, coal from the death of plants, bricks in the shape of teeth.

I begin now to write down all the places I have not been — starting with the most distant.

I build houses that I will not inhabit.

ALISON BUNDY

•°   •

CHIHUAHUA PRIMER

Every person has an idea or two about chihuahuas. Some feel it is proper to dress the creatures in festive, seasonal outfits and invite them up on laps for a visit. Others are concerned about the shape of the chihuahua's skull: its divergence from the common dog skull form causes them worry and even gives a few sensitive souls nightmares. But the chihuahua cannot help it if he has a skull which looks like a simple cap, the type of cap knit by an unpromising beginning knitter.

The chihuahua, like many other dogs, is not allowed to exercise his will very often. This was different, of course, in ancient times, when chihuahuas ran wild in the forests of northern Mexico and burrowed into the ground there in the deep secret folds of nature. Now and then ladies or men, happening by, lost perhaps, or hunting the colorful hypomyces lactifluorum, would catch sight of a chihuahua and they would clap their hands and emit small cries of pleasure, for the little smooth-haired creatures were considered good luck indeed.

And then at some point — it is difficult to say exactly when, history of this sort being always shrouded in darkness —, at some point unknown to most of us but not, one suspects, to the chihuahua, they were lured out of their forests, promised treats, no doubt, caught in cages, ambushed in the dark of night. Their captors may well have had good intentions, may merely have been down on their luck, in need of a charm to start their way back. Such is the attraction of the chihuahua.

We do not, of course, know the names of their captors, but it is a few mere steps from that violent night to this day, when chihuahuas are carried through cities in boxes and bags; dressed in tutus and clown suits and petted unceremoniously by every Tom, Dick, and Harry, as the saying goes; kept on leashes in parks and required to stand on two legs at odd hours of the day and night, waving their front paws helplessly before themselves.

So it is that for some of us, familiar with chihuahua history, a faint coldness clutches the heart when a Lincoln Towncar pulls beside us, carrying a lady who herself carries upon her lap a chihuahua dressed in a miniature and perfect Santa Claus suit. It is winter, snow begins to fall, the chihuahua's tender dark eyes look out and meet ours, and we try to signal to the delicate creature, to put into one glance between species knowledge of a distant and honorable past. But already the car has pulled ahead, is turning, the tiny Santa hat rides out of sight, and we must continue on our way in the snow that is falling everywhere, over houses, cars, and people, over the strange heads of chihuahuas, those beautiful creatures the sight of whom provokes a sense of loss, as they suggest to us another time . . .

STORY OF THE BEEFSTEAK

There it sits. On a plate. The red meat marbled with fat. The light glancing off the white plate.

Who bought the beefsteak? We do not know. Who positioned it thus, on the table?

We do not know. Little beefsteak, give up the answers, tell us your name. Do you recall the field grass bending? How the rain fell down?

ANIMAL LOVER

"Hello quackers," the man called to the ducks. "I have forgotten food for you today — I shall bring it tomorrow," and when he said this he believed himself to be carrying out the mission of St. Francis, even though the language of the birds was denied him, much to his dismay.

He kept the meanest dog. It was little and white and knew how to use its teeth to bite and its claws to scratch him. Masochist, people called him, but it was love and gratitude for attention, not pleasure, which caused him to support the creature's violent behavior. "Each according to his nature," he said when the dog bit his ankle hard and then he would pick up the nasty thing and pop a biscuit in its mouth. He spoke sweet words into the vile pink ear.

Indeed this lover of animals was inconsolable when his bad dog died. He built a little pine coffin and lined it with the softest blanket he could find. He hired a man to engrave the dog's name on a blue flagstone. In his small back yard he dug a hole where the grass met the trees.

Before the burial ceremony could be performed, however, the man threw himself out the third story window. His neighbors did wonder about this: perhaps he had been sitting by the coffin overlong. His sister came to town then and she did a nice thing — she had him buried out back next to the dog. They lowered the little coffin down and then the bigger one, into its hole.

The neighbors wondered some more. Why didn't he just find another dog? Who missed *him* when he was gone? Life has its mysteries. Of course it's a sad story, but what can one do? There will always be some who don't fit into this world.

A SENTIMENTAL MEMORY

I.

In 1925, exactly one decade before my mother was born, the handsome Mosjoukine stood by the sea, ready to enter the Casino and win. I was sitting, at the time, on the marble steps of the Cafe Rialto, facing the boardwalk — an ugly child in an unspeakable white dress and bonnet, playing with painted wooden toys. To be precise, I was two years old, had set the stiff horse in the little yellow cart, and was commencing, in a rage of boredom, to knock him on the snout with a red rectangle. Then M. stopped before me to contemplate the doors that opened to the Casino's hall, and I saw his fine eye fill with integrity and luck. He had a marvelous pallor, and I knew women fell when he walked. The sea extending out behind him seemed nothing when he stood by it, and I felt I was at the boundary of a strange bright land.

Is there a puzzle whose solution is simply the fact of the puzzle's existence? When M. bowed his head slightly and set off toward the Casino, I formed my skirt into a kind of pouch, installed my toys therein, and followed.

II.

Now love is fine, but luck is better. A lucky man gets what he wants and more; he is an emblem of positive possibility. The forest is set up for him to walk through. And, whereas a man in love may dream of his beloved and not notice the passing of time, a man in luck can stop a clock. He is also popular: for, just as luck is his vehicle, so people think he might become their vehicle, and aid them in achieving their myriad desires.

In short, the lesson says a man in luck is a good dream made real. The reason ladies fell before M. was because he produced in them a powerful nostalgia for something they had never had.

III.

So I went into the flamboyant and cruel Casino. A great crowd circulated on the floor, and I became lost in it, emerging some time later, without my toys, onto a small flight of stairs, where I stood taking a view. I could see I was late, but maybe not too late. M. had money stuck in his ears but had not yet turned coy. I had plans to attach myself zealously to him, and cling like a leech, and I started toward his table just as he stood up from it. The ladies clustered about him, but he made his way through. Now is my chance, I thought, and as he came near I lifted my arms and opened my mouth to speak.

At that time, a shadow fell over me, and my heart stopped, and I was unable to say what I had to. I was resuscitated some thirty-six years later, and tell this story not for money, but out of love, and to slow the passing of time somewhat.

PETER GIZZI

•   ••

NEW PICNIC TIME

> *Unless the giddy heaven fall*
> —Andrew Marvell

1.
Out of this close horizon there are animals
breathing unlike a child's drawing of a nativity.
Orbiting circles with brown x's. Farther off
pedestrians make parallel lines and collapse
into distance. Or becoming one of several skylines

in charcoal or finger-paint.

2.
At zero hour an earth unwrites itself.
Becomes an indelible number line
counting backward to embrace its new horizon,
indefatigable zero. The high lit window.
A person tethered to a desk. This city and its outline

its rivers, its cemeteries.

3.
Invisible, the orchard keeper's mansion
is everywhere. The heart becomes one, last stone
of an existing grove and a squatter's earth.
Thus in persons and in plants also stone.
And the brilliant element of fire and to the helix

and throughout the electrics: salt.

4.

Beyond this image decomposing: desire. And as always
with the mouth there is earth. Because it calls, fear is redundant.
And that animal sound in late night is only its own. Speech
becoming one, becoming air, books outlasting buildings
outlast sweat and the broken human form a body labors.

Whose face is the same as another?

5.

Nothing spoke for itself. Every action implied a rhetoric
so it may recognize itself. To teach, to celebrate virtue,
to persuade by example, to lead the court to its ideal self
through wonder. Same page same fable trajectory. A window.
The young father dreaming. A hand a face a feeling.

It was a sound he heard.

6.

The way of earthworms and coffins of dead infants,
cobwebs and deformity, of windows and the children
they expose, the signs they carry (shame),
of sibilants and crossroads. Herein lie the broken,
the sturdy, the well-intentioned policeman.

The smiles they bear across a portal.

7.

When will they say hear me. It was a dream. It was a tin can.
It was a funny thing to feel. And the children. Or beyond this
for posture, a simple garden, evergreen, a green car out front,
the picket fence is white, what color are the flowers
unwritten in a day. There is no space. Only sky and water.

Uncanny earth. A funny thing to feel.

XUE DI

• ••

INTERPLAY

The living
are shadows of the dead
They make noise
When the dead dream in the silent dark
when the dead wake
the living feel sudden terror
day-long loneliness
It is the dead
who have left home
to meet their family on the way
The living, day by day, age
It is the dead who try to
return to the world
The living feel alone
when they meet each other
They shout "Who
loves me?"
It is the dead standing
next to them
The dead clench their teeth
with contempt
with revenge
Because the living
are always giving the dead a bad name

translated by Wang Ping & Keith Waldrop

ANNE-MARIE ALBIACH

•   •   •

INCANTATION

> "I ate from the hand of a God in order to come
> forth and continue on this fractured earth"

She
impregnates my face. Her hair taken, and in the veins addicted blood,
coming from elsewhere, alternate liquid element.

Insidious, she disowns a journey, graphic signs, eyes, in this
meticulous account which no longer frightens them at all.

"memory borrows from flowers and forest such exact art"

On every side strokes appear, whence a voice approaching
incantation.

Billow, obscure destitution, she withdraws into silence, in the least
degree a stranger.

In their childhood, blue cuffs;
"milk of generations"

---

immobility is constrained
it thwarts an otherness and the other's glance connects with
this elaboration.

over the years, a perverse goal's elements.

Such investigation strips bare an indeterminate time, abasing the
relapsed, gestures from this time forward.

Dark shadow lets a body fall, recurring drop into opacity:

> *"the cold is stamped with the sleeper who, roused, restores me to life"*

Three outlines and a pallid erudition. She gives birth in the lineage of
chance; premonition of data: night annihilates objects of an incantatory
solitude, thinned by sleep
"this excitement of the first days"

An illicit body, nudity in the breath.   *They*
hereafter in rumor.

  "at the sight of blood he swooned"

                              They will come no more. In dorsal hues,
they seek each other at break of day.
  I dressed this unprecedented wound in its last stage. The night was
gasping and its fruits even to oblivion. A sketch on the bosom, this color
cast anew on the earth: heat suddenly in the margins. Repetition of
absences
                                          "this complicity
                                  to the point of injury"

translated from the French by Keith Waldrop

GALE NELSON

• • •

SHELVING FIXTURES

resplendent in the active way
of coronation planners. the activist
examined his argumentative spectacle
and changed the color scheme
abruptly. plaster the earrings
into the bathing pools, are
recommended, but were drowned
out by the shouts of the
counter-revolutionaries. what could
we do for the crowned prince
but whisper?

—

anxiety on strings
pardonable excess
charming numericism
abundant largesse fix
sudden silence in a big
frosty glass
arthritic concentration
build the text book thusly
and others amended their bows
sample — glow spew
sharing, gaul spirit
terracing in extremis
solvency excuse
leg   let   spend
  door   door   spew
semb   lack   lad
  tem   tem   put
dove   dove   came
    special   rendering
        pluck   pluck
        spume

the subject reclines
   the object declines
      ampersand consistency
         movement in

carriageway emphasis
   larger constitutional issues
      partridge complacency
         exercise the shattering

a piece of thread

      spittle cup disinterred
         floating island summation

we journey to the lexicon's
retreat, and spark a revolt.
   in the quieter regions
we journey to the syntax
center, and placate the sum.

—

the angle of light has never
been so severe yet we
exude confidence in our driving

we see the exit signs out of
the corner of our eyes and do
our best to keep a steady

distance from other vehicles
severity function is amplified by
our anxiety of serving as judges

in a major competition that may
play out the future for the
participants I am relieved when

the angles shift and only our
ears are super-immersed in sensory
overload

JANE UNRUE

••   •

from: *THE HOUSE*

A painted table, chairs, armchairs and lounge chairs, a bed — all fabricated over galvanized metal tubing — household utensils, linens, clothing and personal articles, shells, bones, flints, pine cones from around the lake: these things were taken in.

By storms or wind the house could be tipped or jolted, caressed, the stretches of the landscape and the slopes and the horizon jagged with mountains and the weight of the atmosphere all concentrating on the house, the depths and the heights of the house remaining, in those ever-changing conditions, fixed, the hard and soft parts remaining fixed, the violence and the gentleness fixed, bringing into the house a kind of happiness (music), or oppression (din or racket, leakage).

A glow fills the air. There is the sound of a motor. An aerial view of a house rapidly receding, clouds blot the scene. A city vanishes. A full noonday sun goes into eclipse. "We're going to the far away shores of island universes in the dark cosmic depths aboard a ship annihilating distances at a speed of some ga-ZILL-ion miles per hour," says an amplified voice. "That out there's the moon, it will become lumpy when the circular craters, mountains, valleys and plains spring into close-up—!" "No, it's the planet Venus," says a second voice, "covered by perpetual—!" "Not Venus," says the first voice, "over there that's Venus, this here is the moon, coming up's the planet—" A shower of meteors like gale-driven luminous snow is swirling all around us. "—Mars, with its polar ice caps, its seas and so-called canals!" But the rings of Saturn are becoming visible: the view is turning earthward. "You bitch," the second voice, "you stupid bitch, you've SCREWED us again!" Clouds flashing over portions of a sphere, squeaks, little sniffy sobs, a brilliant pattern in nearly every color stretches out before us, big sniffs, squeakier sobbing. "I've HAD it with this parade of planets crap," the second voice on top of all that sobbing, "everybody out!"

The house, although I had never seen anything even similar, with the exception of the house to which it was attached, was not the only one. I knew; felt it. But not because the house happened to have been attached to the house next door, although they did appear, at least from their exteriors, to be identical. No, there were littler things than that. In the kitchen (I used to open the little metal door and walk out onto the garden on the roof, looking around at the trees in their pots), instead of the feeling that should come from knowing in the dark where everything is that's in your kitchen, I would sometimes get a feeling that somewhere, in another house, I might have found the exact same configuration of conveniences (I used to lie back in the bed and look up): ventilation fans to waste disposal unit to recessed refrigerator-freezer to electric cooker to the recessed stove; storage cupboards side by side flanking a triple sink across from the recessed stove; the overhead glass rack; a painted table in the center; fold-away counter tops, peripherally.

The staircase was illuminated by a wall of glass bricks that switched on automatically, the timer having been concealed behind glass brick A-32—there was a number on the back of each glass brick matching the number in the slot for each glass brick telling me, when came time to put a glass brick back, where in the wall of them I was. And this glass brick — there was a light bulb behind each glass brick, except for the one that had the timer behind it — had had in front of it, sometimes spilling over to 30 and 31, B-32, C-32, B-30 and 29, and sometimes, depending on the breadth of leaves, as far over and up as C-31 or B-28, ever since move-in, a truly hairy-looking plant, hidden behind the staircase but not entirely hidden from any sunlight coming in.

A table for working or eating, chairs and armchairs of different dimensions, lounge chairs, door and window frames, steps, handles for opening the drawers and the storage cupboards in the kitchen, a bed, and some of the corresponding materials such as folded sheet metal and galvanized metal tubing, welding: furniture, and all of the other elements designed and put together for a lifetime of functions to be carried out more comfortably and efficiently than ever had been possible in the past; while the sun, also for a lifetime of functions that are regular — the continents not sinking, ice not shifting on the water — moved as if too heavy for its job of passing over a house tat was, supposedly, all proportion. And, in fact, at times, for instance, when looking in a drawer, or at my reflection in a window, or just when walking down the steps leading from the terrace into the grass — yes, at times it did feel as if it had been designed for no one other than myself.

That — that is too much to have to live with.

ERNST JANDL

• • •

CHANSON

l'amour
die tür
the chair
der bauch

the chair
die tür
l'amour
der bauch

der bauch
die tür
the chair
l'amour

l'amour
die tür
the chair

le tür
d'amour
der chair
the bauch

le chair
der tür
die bauch
th'amour

le bauch
th'amour
die chair
der tür

l'amour
die tür
the chair

am'lour
tie dür
che thair
ber dauch

tie dair
che lauch
am thür
ber'dour

che dauch
am'thour
ber dür
tie lair

l'amour
die tür
the chair

E. J.

DILECTION
some think
terring reft flom light
is a piece of cake.
boy are they evel
long!

Anselm Hollo

```
   o
fr  sch      i
 i      ch  mp
  E. J.    o
```
Ben Friedlander

CANZONE   MEDIEVAL

ganz	'mid
ganz	'mid
ohne	evil
völlig beraubt	no good

canzone	medieval

ganz	'mid
ganz	'mid
ohne	evil
völlig beraubt	no good

E. J.   *Gale Nelson*

COUNT
done
noose
free
nor
live
nix
never
fate
whine
then

James Sherry

GESTURES: A GAME
ANGLICAN
for a piss-hop

```
    bluesy
   b  lues   y
  b   lues     y
 b    lues       y
              E. J.
```

A ROMANCE
```
     frank
     f ran k
    f  ran   k
   f   ran     k
       after
       sally
      s all y
     s  all   y
    s   all     y
       day
```
Brian Schorn

```
MY     : T
       :
liber  : tea
       :
[fr]   :
eterni : tee
       :
[equ]  :
all a  : tease
       :
```
Craig Watson

from: **"the big e"**

e) even sex-hexed men mend nets
    even zen-spent men need mend
    even elf-seen men bend necks
    even sex-flecked men's seeds fend
    even zen-helped men breed sex seeds
    even elf-helped men tend wrecks
    even sex-hexed men mend nets

e) errers err re errers
    e'en ere errers err errers erst err'd
    e'en ere errers stretch erect extended
    fete genteel genes effete
    vexed errers better stet bedwetters err'r
    lest vexed errers kept stetted ere bedwetters get better

e) ever seek ether
    needles even seek ether-seekers
    needles even seek ether needle-seekers seek
    ether evens eden
    ether evens needle-eden
    ether needles ethers even eden-needles seek
    ether greets lechers
    lechers enter
    lechers enter needles even
    lechers enter needle-ether
    lechers enter eden

e) sweet herbs sweeten sweeter elements
    wet stems whet nettles' wetter welt
    tethers tethered tetherers' tenderer elements
    effected stretches reflect defect tenements
    quellers squelch quellers' nerve-swell
    sellers sell cells' nerve-swelled whey
    hell's belt held helen's element
    feller's press'd-festered neck festers best

Guy Bennet

202

EMMANUEL HOCQUARD

• •   •

from: *A TEST OF SOLITUDE: Sonnets*

I

At Christmas, Cyrille brought the wolves into
the house.
Where does he find them.
They sing for forty minutes
at the bitching hour.
Part of a pack echoes scraps of distance
Ever since I've listened to them for several
These wolves, Viviane, sing around the points.
Must they enter the room for us to hear the snow
falling.
Heaps of little lives in juxtaposition.
If I wrote to *you* in the past tense I would feel I
was lying.
Will you be back on New Year's Day?

II

What empties a name of its substance.
What kind of grammar would a grammar with-
out questions be
and what are the questions about.
You are not a question, but surrounded by kinds
of questions.
Is it snowing how do wolves howl.
Yes, Viviane.
Not answering any question
could one say that yes and to be are one.
Now yes.
"I felt I understood."
Yes
could be the missing word.

III

Viviane is Viviane, yes.
Tautology does not say all but yes.
Yes and all are not equivalents. Every yes fills
the space of language, which for all that does not
form a whole.
One would not obtain a sum by adding up these
yeses.
What if we subtracted *all* from our vocabulary.
Those wolves do not sing in chorus.
The space filled by their scraps of voices is a
broken space.
Heaps of little spaces in juxtaposition
sing
around the points.

XXV

I write that in order to write this. What is written
is so twice over.
What *you* read, is it two?
Between two there is a field whose form turns
between us.
This hole is boundless.
Around this hole, the song of the birds
comprehends day breaks on one 11th of April.
Night is contained in the silence of the black and
white goat is dead.
The lines of words are folded this way.
There is no end to two remain
or Viviane the price to pay.
Grammar and fiction are one.

translated from the French by Rosmarie Waldrop

CROSSCUT UNIVERSE:
WRITING ON WRITING FROM FRANCE

•   •**•**

Dominique Fourcade •
THE SENTENCE

The sentence always translated from an other language, the sentence unfounded, the sentence of liquid shadows beyond which we do not look, writing it,

Joseph Guglielmi •
ABIOGRAPHY

> Biography, title first chosen then rejected with spirit, but recovered with a new meaning, full and even redundant, since life could never be separated from writing.
>
> (Roger Laporte)

> how read it
> line after line
> given
> one look
> refresh the eyes
> against the abyss
> (Larry Eigner)

How to read Roger Laporte's book *Fugue*? And why borrow this question from Larry Eigner, if not to suggest that here, as there, a game is in play which reduces the page to "ruined archival theater".... Here and there "another time" (keeping in mind that *another time in fragments* is the title of a Larry Eigner book) invents itself whose *fragmentary power* reaffirms the inextinguishable creativity of human language, the inexhaustible "fountain of youth," the forever-knotted Reverdian *"thread of ink"* whose tangles

> . . . refresh the eyes
> against the abyss. . .

Network of fragmentary/fragmenting strength and *empty border bordering the void* (stands up *against?* *against the abyss*), in Laporte and in Eigner, two modes appear to undermine the continuity, the density of discourse, both *(both)* beginning from *(from)* the enigmatic *evidence* (word resembling — let's quickly say it *as a practical joke* — the perfect stencilo of *(emptiness)* of what can happen during the work of writing, i.e. the incoercible exfoliation of the blackened leaf, the *biographical (Life scatters its lesson)* documentary pulverization, where *"time changes at the opening of a new calendar."*

Here, delicately trapped by one of the most dramatic auto-designations, there, inscribed *with* anecdote itself and in the midst of its *marginal* suspension *(projective/fall forward)*, the *new biography,* major biography, "this superexistence" asserts itself (without telling) be it by the transformation of its means of distribution, be it by the (endless) exploding of its text field, thus subverted...

How to read "this ellipse of history"?
these "forests of possibility"?
How to read these two *(projective)* celebrations of the weave, these conjugations of "vanishing lines" sustained by who knows what "fearful symmetry"?

Emmanuel Hocquard •
from: *THIS STORY IS MINE:*
Little Autobiographical Dictionary of Elegy

Pretty soon I heard whimpering.
James Durham, *Dark Window*

AH!  ALAS!

The classical elegy, as it was taught to us (poem expressing regret, lament (V. *that word*), sadness, melancholy, pain, nostalgia, etc.) obeys the following schema: *it had begun well; time passed; and, in the end, it went bad.*

1st column: **Ah!**	*time passes*	2nd column: **Alas!**
I had some great times with Cynthia.	⟶	Today I am miserable because Cynthia is totally frivolous.
I was happy in Rome, surrounded by friends and covered in laurels.	⟶	Now I am all alone and sad in my exile in Romania.
Myrto shipped out, content to be on her way to marry in Camarine.	⟶	Alas, the ship sank, and Myrto drowned.

If Propertius and Ovid take us into their confidence, and Chenier on the other hand brings us tabloid news, in every instance it is a question of the lyric amplification of an anecdotal situation (V. **Anecdote**). And when, as at the piano, one presses all the way down on the hyperbolic pedal of elegiac representation, one achieves pathos.

To summarize: in the beginning, *tout va bien*. Then things spoil. Elegiac time flows in this direction: *Hélas pour moi!*

Jacques Roubaud •
from: *POÉSIE, ETCETERA: MÉNAGE*

2 — Nations, Poetry

At times, in some countries, distant or near, someone asks, "Is there a French poetry?"

(meaning, "Is there still poetry in France?" (meaning, "You know very well (your newspapers themselves are full of it), there is no more literature in France. And you're French! And you call yourself a poet! How do you explain this?) — what could I answer? I don't answer at all)

More generally, if X is a country, what does "the poetry of X" mean?

3 — Eine Nationale Poesie?

@1

@1.1 In my family, the telephone made no inroad until 1945. I was twelve. It was a strange and formidable apparatus, a kind of divinity, undoubtedly hostile. My father did not wish to answer its call, even less to initiate its use. It was my mother's job to exorcise it. But even she must not have really succeeded in mastering it. In fact, several years having gone by, we had left Carcassonne where we had lived for the entire war (let me remind you that there was a war from 1939 to 1945), we had come to Paris to live and one day my mother received a phone call from an old friend from back there, from before. They spoke for a moment, exchanged news about family, children, and when they were about to hang up my mother said, "Let's not let so much time go by without speaking. Take my telephone number." "Yes, you're right, give it to me," the friend began to say. At that moment they both broke into laughter.

@1.2 As for myself, I have not progressed very much in the mastery of this instrument. And, when I received a call from Hamburg asking me the title for my talk for today, I had a moment of panic. Thinking of the unbelievable distance traveled by the voice arriving invisibly at my ear, I answered bluntly, with hesitation in voice and ear, "a national poetry?" And so this is how the title occurred to me, practically illiterate in German matters, in a kind of German, something I find well adapted; and thus subsequently I adopt "Eine nationale Poesie?" pronouncing it my way.

@1.3 I will proceed in the following manner. First I will question the idea of nation. Secondly I will ask myself what poetry can have to do with nation. I will stay more or less in an interrogatory mode, having few answers to bring forward; which will not prevent me from expressing myself peremptorily, like everyone else.

@2
@2.1 For some years, France, eager to indicate it harbors no ill will towards Germany for certain misunderstandings arisen in their recent common history, has borrowed their concept of a political movement with fascist tendencies called the *Front National* whose leader (there has to be a leader) is named Le Pen.

@2.2 One of the strong ideas of the *Front National* is "France for the French!" or "Stick together and our cows will be kept safe!" There are too many foreigners in France, they say, they are invading us, like the Arabs long ago, conquered by Charles Martel (an honorary member of the *Front National*) in Poitiers in 732. They eat our bread, break into our security and our social security. In short, "They leap into our arms / massacre our children and our mates." At least symbolically.

@2.3 So we must get rid of the foreigners.

@2.4 At this moment we encounter a problem. If we send these foreigners back to their homeland, it means we can distinguish them in a clear and indisputable way from the French, who must remain home. Good. What is a French person?

@2.5 Laboring over the question, the *Front National,* in the voice of its leader (there has to be a leader speaking in everyone's name) has proposed a definition of a French person.

@2.6 Le Pen's Definition: **He or she whose parents are both French is French.**

@2.7 Enthusiastic about this definition, I composed the following poem, already translated into a number of languages, I say proudly (this does not happen to me very often), including German.

@2.8 Attention: the poem must be read very fast!

@2.9. Poem:

Is Le Pen French?

If Le Pen were French according to Le Pen's definition, that would mean that, according to Le Pen's definition, Le Pen's mother and Le Pen's father would have been themselves French according to Le Pen's definition, which would mean that, according to Le Pen's definition, Le Pen's mother's mother, as well as Le Pen's mother's father as well as Le Pen's father's mother not to forget Le Pen's father's father would have been, according to Le Pen's definition, French, and it follows that Le Pen's mother's mother's mother as well as that of Le Pen's mother's father as well as that of Le Pen's father's mother, and that of Le Pen's father's father would have been French according to Le Pen's definition; and by the same token, and for the same reason, Le Pen's mother's mother's father, as well as that of Le Pen's mother's father as well as that of Le Pen's father's mother, and that of Le Pen's father's father would have been French, always according to the same definition, that of Le Pen

whence one will deduce with no trouble and without the help of Le Pen, following this reasoning

either there is an infinite number of French people who were born French according to Le Pen's definition, who lived and died French according to Le Pen's definition since the dawn of the beginning of time or else

Le Pen is not French according to Le Pen's definition.

Jacques Roubaud, Provençal

@2.10 I had to sign "Provençal," not being French myself but more or less Provençal, in any case I am if you go back a few generations. (I would gladly place the troubadour Rubaut among my ancestors, but I have not succeeded in determining as yet all the missing links in my genealogy.)

@2.11 The second branch of the alternative, namely that Le Pen is not French according to his own definition received stunning confirmation recently. While in New York for a reading at the Poetry Project at Saint Mark's Place, and after I read my poem, someone brought me a pen with the brand name Le Pen. Examining it I saw that it was "made in Japan." Quod erat demonstrandum.

translated from the French by Norma Cole

SUSAN GEVIRTZ

•• •

HYPHEN'S HYPHEN

Nothing is thought

or what we
thought

I stayed out of your body

to let it air

but the air would not

I stayed out of the air

to let the body

but avail
not

The unopened room in which the tide had gone out exposing miles
of floor never before seen

Where there is everything

is never there

what in the world

        susceptible to the call

to mean an order
                it orders

hostage time

How continue
where there is no

outside

proximity's estuary

before
incident, arrival. Sojourn in matter. The sun's mind. Kymatik.
Isn't musical experience

outside sound's
light

drop song

a phenomenon keeps watch on itself

scouring the seabed

for unforseen

We enter the epoch

And nothing will stay stay

nothing left

was

nothing

last

OSKAR PASTIOR

•   ••

O MAGDALEN!

The town in which my capacity for thought is
frittered away is a large, proud, round town.
The thought of horse is not, e.g. part of it.

This town which is my one and all consisting of
two halves of Merseburg is called also Merseburg,
because, even if I do think of horse, something

not part of it, maybe, my one and all is dimin-
ished in it; and consists of two large, proud
hemispheres, because these hemispheres fall

apart if my horses run out of breath. Right
there at the gates of my town, which gates are
held together by spells, there the horses sweat

and strain. They use up a lot of breath. When
Merseburg falls apart at both Merseburg gates,
it is either daytime or it is night. I

need day as well as night time for thinking —
which makes me run out of breath. My town in
which breath runs out combines not only phy-

sics, but also the horses, to think of which is
not part of it — they heave and split, it's
then I think that my capacity for thought runs

out. When the proud hemispheres fall apart, I
think, even the proud words run out of force
and one and all depart — to the northnorthsouth.

translated from the German by Christopher Middleton

214

ABRACADABRA

abracadabra as was
tartar, as was kandahar-
cardan (tack that man and gal
flat as washrags!), as was cash
cadav-bag, as was macad-
am-madam, and Kamchatka
(that anagram was banal)

perfect steel fetters defend
the element's element,
when even pesterers (beep-
beep, beep-beep!) engender these
deepened well-essences; then
nettlebeds redeem the hell
where chester cheeses breed (bet?)

if in wilds iltis is striv-
ing with sissi — is it im-
pinging? Inspiring tri-mi-
ni-kids. Sissi's rimini-
kilt-itch stirs him. In this biz,
big risk: in hindsight it's tick-
lish, Sissi's biting "finish!

no-color o-moo-cocoon
spools pro lotto for wood-rod:
on spot of god pollock's cold,
chloroform stops motor-knock,
solo moons don't brood, or prows
slow-cook loco (on dock) — or
songs bow down to protocol

ur-cur trusts sulfur tubs: plush
cult buff. up church hulk, duck hung —
bull guru struck dun — glum slump
turns, unstuck sulk burns: tumult
trust sunk! ruth hums, plumb tug un-
stuck, truthful-dumb bunk-buzz. sum
up? just cuscus rush; just rush!

translated by Harry Mathews

IRREVERSIBLE? IS TIME — were it as itself — reading underneath the influence of palindromitis? Or what is it, earlier or later, with or without authority, that probably determines orientation — and beats the record? Perhaps without memory and imagination; nevertheless this is something no-one says. Therefore syntax solely noway works it. No money as consolation or innocence imprisoned — mere relationship. Against vagueness, reading too quickly thereby creates otherwise former procedure as rewind. And definitely bending sentences snip syllables wherever it is heading. Aha! *heading*, is it? Wherever syllables snip sentences (bending definitely!) and rewind as procedure (former "otherwise") creates "thereby" — quickly, too. Reading vagueness "against" relationship, mere imprisoned innocence, or consolation as money? No! it works. Noway solely syntax. Therefore (says no-one), something is this nevertheless: imagination and memory, without "perhaps," record the beats, and orientation determines (probably) that authority, without or with (later or earlier) "it is." What "or" (palindromitis) of influence, the underneath? Reading itself, as it were, time is irreversible.

translated by Harry Mathews

BLE

(for franz mon 1986)

when the parade horse horses through the parade
and dise like digms abound in ox

when llels lipomena go to the pet in guay
with noia meters pluie and sol

O clete — then ffin phrases phernalia
(bles of plegiac keets troop to the llax)

because the gon must chute and feed the sites
and bolicly the graph rides lysis to the mount

translated by Rosmarie Waldrop

216

WHAT, HOWEVER, IS the discretion of left to your? What is never needed by ominable ab? Would swum have? Too pensive for ex? Suction-cupped over? Bogeymanhole conspiracy? And why where?

WITH BRASS AND BAND, tinnitus on the Rhine. It's no carnival, it's no overall, it's nothing but a dragon-green earwig — and merry free-for-all!... we hear so much about the Rhine. My father who a foxtail was, my mother who a woolfish was, all Greek to me a mouse king was — and it's all tinnitus to me... By hearsay tinnitus is an asparagus-hyacinth. Its hammer that an anvil was, its anvil that a jammer was, its stir up — Pig Latin. Its grammar has behindhand bracketed its iamb... Bubbles are rising, tandaradei. Tinnitus brassy and randy: cut class! cut class!

BEERY CYCLING, HOARY TRAIN, airy flex! Hairy moulade, leary dundancy, dairy busses — nary an armament of mince, marmalade blocks story sistance in the square.... On all fours gory mates dinary animals from Addis Abeba to Fürth. The barker the birch the stunger the bung — headwind, steady tory proaches. For ordinarks are neither handy tectives nor show ordinary spect: antiphlox, ilophone...

IT'S ON DRY COHESION that the army surgeon pins his handkerchief complete with bread-and-butter smell. A giant pencase with snowy circles chains the cactus to the pier — approximating sundried apples. No rebus that would shrink, but 56 strokes per minute (sardines in oil) equal precisely the fraction of a mile... let us now take to heart along the hill with sawed-off shotguns, and from iodine and evil flee into our washbags briefly — at the expense of sunset red, the surgeon makes himself scarce brownstone: O hair curlers... let us together lean against hydrants, horny infants, seals, pompous messages on tallow, toast and rifle up to the remote cuntrol of crosshair mass for which all seven lines — his handkerchief is steamy.

translated by Rosmarie Waldrop

217

PASCAL QUIGNARD

•.   •

from; *ON WOODEN TABLETS: APRONENIA AVITIA*

CHAPTER FIVE
(folio 500 recto to folio 505 verso)

LXXIV. A Memory of Q. Alcimius

On the Quirinal, Quintus knocked faintly, four times, on the shutter. I opened the door. His clothes were wet with fog. He put his arms about me. With a smile I said, take your cloak [*paenula*] off. His hair was all mussy and raindrops hung there like drops clinging to ferns. He asked for a change of linen. There was no fire-pan in the room. I took off his clothes, rubbing him dry. His toes and fingers were still ice-cold. He put his mouth to my ear and whispered a vulgarity, and suddenly I felt light-hearted, full of life.

LXXV. Things Not to Forget

The mallow laxatives.
A bath-caldron.

LXXVI. Things Not to Forget

At the baths of Titus.

LXXVII. Description of Winter

I like the bracing cold of winter, rain-free, without fog, and footsteps sounding along the lanes.
Hoarfrost on roofs and marble statues.
Hoarfrost on the done-up hair of women servants.
The unmitigated cruelty of light.
Clouds of breath exhaled by children, animals, men, little slaves hacking out ice-chunks.

I like to see charcoal burning in fire-pans, bodies turning to them. Different parts of the body moving into them, from desire or whim.

LXXVIII. Catarrhs

Awful catarrhs. My left forehead throbbing in pain. A cough keeps me awake. Publius Saufeius comes to see me. I can't get my breath.

"There's a trace of ash in your heart," he says. "What we've been through, together — it's not utterly consumed. A trace of ash in your heart impedes your breathing."

LXXIX. What P. Saufeius Minor Said

P. Saufeius's head was wrapped in a blue woolen bandage. He had a yellow hood over it. I coughed. Spatale brought in herbal tea, the mulled wine. Marulla poured oil into lamps. The sky was inky, like an octopus all of a sudden shooting black. I couldn't stop coughing. Publius coughed himself. I remembered Spurius. I spoke of dying.

"There's no need to be frightened," Publius told me. "I'll be the first to be straw-man.* It's all of our fate. To get tossed into the arena of the dead."

LXXX. Things Not to Forget

In April she'll cross the Tiber at Porto.

LXXXI. Things to Remember

Soles of old shoes falling apart in the mud.

-----

*A pun on "prima pila." Referring to the first dummy thrown to bulls in the ring, to goad them on. Consequently, torn to pieces. Metaphorically "prima pila" means a rag, a dust rag

LXXXII. *Signs of Happiness*

Signs of happiness — inherited wealth.
Precision in language, an accent that consists in not having an accent.
A park with variety and shade and rolling hills.
Physical robustness.
A variety of friends, loquacious, knowing how to read. But also the indulgent guest who on occasion can slip easily into vulgarity.
The face of a man whose eyes reflect a whole range of emotion like mirrors from Levant.
Sleeping five hours as long as it's uninterruped.
The company of a man fond of pleasure — meaning pleasure as a type of good manners.
A moderate fear, in response to death.
Taking a bath.
Using the lyre.

LXXXIII. *Something Sp. Possidius Barca Used to Say*

Spurius said — and was this 10 or 13 harvests ago — he could stick Publius's ass inside Marius's and would anything be left?

LXXXIV. *Happiness*

Happiness. Wandering the Saburnian road.
The eleventh hour. Gossip. Merchants closing up.
Receiving the Vitellian tablets.
Drunkenness before sleep.

LXXXV. *Things Not to Forget*

Pennyroyal against coughing.
The mallow emollients.
Sassina cheeses.

LXXXVI. Epigram of P. Saufeius Minor

Publius formulated this epigram on M. Pollio's cowardly behavior —
"On all fours, he laps up the dog's water."

LXXXVII. What Nasica Smells Like

Nasica comes to see me. On the advice of Melania, Nasica turned
Christian, was anointed by the sacrificer, and was given the name
Paulina. I tell her suddenly:
"You smell quite strongly. Consult Sotodes."
Paulina maintains that a virgin's body can be given to the curious and
sometimes immodest motions of cleansing at most once a week. "This
body of filth," says Paulina. Laughingly, I say, one look at you convinces
me of that! I don't ask for details about a whim she has, ill-befitting a
body reserved for gods, untouched, shedding layers of filth. When
Paulina sits down, why does she dust off the seat she's about to sit on?
She should dust off her own rear-end before sitting.

LXXXVIII. Things Not to Forget

Pennyroyal for coughs
Sassina cheese.

LXXXIX. Sickness of Sp. Possidius Barca

I had the slaves take a folding bed and open it beside Spurius. He was
drooling. I bent over. He smelled like decay, like a chick hatching out of
an egg. I sat on the edge of the folding bed and rested my hand on my
husband's chest. I told him, you stink like a dead dog. He said — "to
remind you of little Muola's furry odor." He added — "you don't have
to put yourself to the trouble of visiting me like this or at least you don't
need to stay so long at the end of the day. " I said:
"I'll stop coming the day you smell like the farts of an Egyptian
hippopotamus."
Spurius had the good grace to laugh. Later, I took from Mommeius's
hands the large basin he intended to put under his master's mouth.
Assisted by Spatale, helping him sit up, I stuck my finger into his mouth

to make him vomit. At the first watch he dozed. I stayed near and told the slave to go get Sotodes. I consulted him. I had him show me the urine and feces of the day. Cladus prepared a horoscope.

At nightfall, after the oil lamps were filled and put up on the walls, after Spatale, Flaviana, Marulla and myself had washed Spurius's body using a sponge soaked in solution of myrrh, milk and foliat, stammering and prompted by a sudden whim, Spurius asks to have his clients, servants and slaves withdraw. Even Flaviana has to go. He settles down. He speaks to me for some time, although he becomes more and more incoherent, babbling, like a child. I bend over not so much to hear what he's saying, but to listen to the drone of that voice in which gentleness and the weakness of death had imperceptibly joined sleep's stupor.

Spurius spoke of journeys we'd planned for the summer. I slipped my fingers into his hands. It's hard for me to recognize my husband — in the large, aged, naked, pink, depilated, wrinkled body, glistening with sweat. I see an awkward body rolled in fetal position, sucking up fear like mother's milk and drowsing off. For a moment I study him, as he sleeps soundly. What's so surprising is, with left hand already consigned to Rhadamantes, and right to Eachus, the crown of the skull caught in Charu's net, denying the obvious — he'd think of his sickness as only temporary, not feel the death already touching him. At dinner I had murene filets, sow-nipple points, grilled clams, sugar beets, and two *setiers* of dark thick wine of Opimius.

XC. *Sickness of Sp. Possidius Barca*

A man who, during life, worries about his health, his porcelain teeth, his oncoming old age and death in deaths of friends. This man refuses to see his own death. He suddenly expects remission. He multiplies plans made ridiculous by the state of his body. He dins this into the ears of a woman who knows its hopelessness.

A man who confuses what's actually a viper's body — with the reflection of the bow he carries.

XCI. *Things to Do*

Cinnamon and balm.

XCII. Death of Sp. Possidius Barca

He stammers out the name Gabba, then says a few things lacking coherence. As Leitus and Philo apply poultices to the legs and as, with Spatale's help, Flaviana makes final preparations for the pennyroyal in the goblet, he turns his face to me, searching with his eyes, gently raising those eyebrows, smiling a bit, his face more distant, more unhappy. I put my hand into his. We all go about our business silently. Marulla pours oil in the lamps. A little gurgling noise catches in Spurius's throat. As if caught by a mute contagion, one after another, we come to a complete halt. Then we weep and wail.

XCIII. Things That Smell Good

Myrtle.
A red saffron from Corycos.
The aroma of blossoming vine.
Ground-up amber.
Nard and myrrh to make foliat.

XCIV. Things Not to Forget

Juice from the Chelidonian isles.
8 balls of aphronite.

XCV. Things to Do

Interest due on the Kalends.

XCVI. Bags of Gold

24 bags of gold.

XCVII. A Thing Said by Sp. Possidius Barca

After Spurius died, nothing particular came to mind. This morning I thought of something he said on his deathbed, that moved me:
"There's not another life. We won't see each other again."
Our tears fell. We held hands.

translated from the French by Bruce X

Contents:
A Century in Two Decades
A Burning Deck Anthology 1961-1981

Bibliography 1981-2001

(• = still in print)

100. **John Yau**, *Broken Off By the Music* (poems). 54 pp. Text linotyped in 12 pt. Devinne. Designed and printed letterpress on Warren's Olde Style by Rosmarie Waldrop, with the title and half titles in 2 colors. Offset cover by Keith Waldrop. 6x9, perfectbound paperback. 950 copies. Providence, 1981. ISBN 0-930900-96-0

100a. Same. Cloth. 50 numbered & signed copies. ISBN 0-930900-95-2

101. • *A Century in Two Decades* (anthology). 176 pp. Text linotyped in 10 pt. Caledonia. Designed and printed letterpress on Warren's Olde Style by Rosmarie Waldrop, with the title and half title pages in 2 colors. Offset cover by Keith Waldrop. 6x9, smyth-sewn paperback. 1400 copies. Providence, 1982. ISBN 0-930901-01-0

101a. Same. Cloth. 100 numbered & signed copies. ISBN 0-930901-00-2

102. **Anthony Barnett**, *A Forest Utilization Family* (poems). 30 pp. Handset in 12 & 18 pt. Caslon Oldstyle, designed and printed letterpress on Warren's Olde Style by Pitt Harding. 2-color title page. 6-1/4x9-1/2, saddle-stitched, in Classic Laid wrappers. 475 copies, of which 26 are lettered and signed. Providence, 1982. ISBN 0-930901-08-8

102a. • Same. 26 lettered & signed copies.

103. **Ray Ragosta**, *Sherds* (poems). 30 pp. Text linotyped in 12 pt. Palatino. Designed and printed letterpress on Warren's Olde Style by Doretta Wildes, with the title page in 2 colors. 6-1/4x9-1/2, saddlestitched, in Classic Laid wrappers. 474 copies. Providence, 1982. ISBN 0-930901-08-8

103a. • Same. 26 lettered & signed copies.

104. **Dallas Wiebe**, *The Transparent Eye-Ball & Other Stories*. 114 pp. Text lino-typed in 10 pt. Palatino. Designed by Keith Waldrop (using a photo of the author by William Hamrick). Printed letterpress on Warren's Olde Style by Rosmarie Waldrop, with the title page and 4 half titles in 2 colors. 5x7-1/4 Perfectbound. 950 copies. Providence, 1982. ISBN 0-930900-92-8

104a. Same. Cloth. 50 numbered & signed copies. ISBN 0-930900-91-x

105. • **Tom Ahern**, *Superbounce* (short short stories). 28 pp. Text linotyped in 12 pt. Palatino with handset titles. Designed and printed letterpress on Warren's Antique by Jennifer Montgomery, with the title page in 2 colors. 6-1/4x9-1/2, saddlestitched, in Strathmore Grandee wrappers. 474 copies. Providence, 1983.ISBN 0-930901-12-6

105a. • Same. 26 lettered & signed copies.

106.   **Deirdra Baldwin,** *Totemic* (poems). 32 pp. Text linotyped in 11 pt. Caledonia with handset titles. Designed and printed letterpress on Warren's Olde Style by Pitt Harding. 2 colors throughout. 6-1/4x9-1/2, saddle stitched, in Artemis wrappers. 474 copies. Providence, 1983.ISBN 0-930901-13-4

106a•   Same. 26 lettered & signed copies.

107. •   **Mei-mei Berssenbrugge,** *The Heat Bird* (poems). 64 pp.Text linotyped in 11 pt. Caledonia. Designed and printed letterpress on Warren's Olde Style by Rosmarie Waldrop, with the title page and 4 half titles in 2 colors. The cover reproduces an etching by Lee Sherry and Porfirio DiDonna. 6x9, smyth-sewn paperback. 950 copies. Providence, 1982. ISBN 0-930901-03-7

107a.   Same. Cloth. 50 numbered & signed copies. ISBN 0-930901-02-9

108.   **Nancy Condee,** *Explosion in the Puzzle Factory* (poems). 28 pp. Text linotyped in 12 pt. Palatino with handset titles. Designed and printed letterpress on Warren's Olde Style by Pitt Harding. 2-color title page. 6-1/4x9-1/2, saddlestitched, in Strathmore wrappers. 474 copies. Providence,1983. ISBN 0-930901-18-5

108a.•   Same. 26 lettered & signed copies.

109.   **Robert Coover,** *In Bed One Night & Other Brief Encounters* (stories). 64 pp. Text linotyped in 10 pt. Palatino with hand-set titles. Design and offset cover by Keith Waldrop, with title and half titles in 2 colors. 5x7-1/4, smyth-sewn paperback. 1000 copies. Providence, 1983. ISBN 0-930901-17-7

109a.   Same. Cloth. 200 numbered & signed copies.ISBN 0-930901-16-9

110.   **Michael Gizzi,** *Species of Intoxication* (poems). 76 pp. Text linotyped in 11 pt. Caledonia. Designed and printed letterpress on Warren's Olde Style by Rosmarie Waldrop, with the title page in 2 colors. Offset cover by Keith Waldrop. 6x9, smyth-sewn paperback. 950 copies. Providence, 1983. ISBN 0-930901-11-8

110a.   Same. Cloth. 50 numbered & signed copies. ISBN 0-930901-10-x

111.   **Christopher Middleton,** *Woden Dog* (poems). 20 pp. Text linotyped in 12 pt. Palatino. Designed by Keith Waldrop. Printed letterpress on Warren Olde Style by Rosmarie Waldrop. 2 colors throughout. 6-1/4x9-1/2, saddlestitched, in Strathmore wrappers. 474 copies. Providence, 1983. ISBN 0-930901-07-x

111a.•   Same. Printed on Barcham Green Charter Oak, handsewn, in Fabriano wrappers. 26 lettered & signed copies. ISBN 0-930901-06-1

112. •   **W.D.Snodgrass,***Six Minnesinger Songs* (texts & music). 48 pp. Text linotyped in 11 pt. Caledonia with titles in Caslon Oldstyle. Designed by Keith Waldrop. Printed letterpress on Warren Olde Style by Rosmarie Waldrop, with the title and half titles pages in 2 colors. 6-1/4x9-1/2, saddlestitched, in Artemis wrappers. 1000 copies. Providence, 1983. ISBN 0-930901-05-3

112a.   Same. Printed on Barcham Green Charter Oak, handsewn, in Fabriano wrappers. 26 lettered & signed copies. ISBN 0-930901-04-5

113.•   **Keith Waldrop,** *The Space of Half an Hour* (poems). 88 pp. Text linotyped in 12 pt. Palatino with handset titles. Designed and printed letterpress on Warren's Olde Style by Rosmarie Waldrop, with the title and half titles in 2 colors. Offset cover by the author. 6x9, smyth-sewn paperback. 1450 copies. Providence,1983. ISBN 0-930901-20-7

113a.   Same. Cloth. 50 numbered & signed copies. ISBN 0-930901-19-3

114.	**C. K. Williams,** *The Lark. The Thrush. The Starling* (poems after Issa). 32 pp. Text linotyped in 14 pt.Caledonia. Designed and printed letterpress on Warren's Olde Style by Rosmarie Waldrop. 2 colors throughout. The cover reproduces a drawing by the author. 6-1/4x9-1/2, saddlestitched, in Strathmore wrappers. 500 copies. Providence, 1983. ISBN 0-930901-15-0

114a.	Same. On Barcham Green Charter Oak, handsewn, in Fabriano wrappers. 23 lettered & signed copies. ISBN 0-930901-14-2

115. •	**Rae Armantrout,** *Precedence* (poems). 48 pp. Text linotyped in 12 pt. Palatino with handset titles. Designed and printed letterpress on Warren's Olde Style by Rosmarie Waldrop, with the title and half title in 2 colors. Offset cover by Keith Waldrop, using a photograph by the author. 6x9, smyth-sewn paperback. 950 copies. Providence, 1985. ISBN 0-930901-24-x

115a.	Same. Cloth. 50 numbered & signed copies. ISBN 0-930901-23-1

116.•	**Michael Davidson,** *The Landing of Rochambeau* (poems). 80 pp. Text linotyped in 11 pt. Caledonia. Designed and printed letterpress on Warren's Olde Style by Rosmarie Waldrop, with the title and half title in 2 colors. Offset cover by Keith Waldrop, using a US postage stamp. 6x9, smyth-sewn paperback. 900 copies. Providence, 1985. ISBN 0-930901-26-6

116a.	Same. Cloth. 100 numbered & signed copies. ISBN 0-930901-25-8

117.•	**John Hawkes,** *Innocence in extremis* (novella). 100 pp. Text linotyped in 10 pt. Palatino. Designed and printed letterpress on Warren's Olde Style by Brita Bergland, with the title page in 2 colors. Cover photograph by Ruby Ray. 5x7-1/4, smyth-sewn paperback. 2000 copies. Providence, 1985. ISBN 0-930901-30-4

117a.	Same. Cloth. 500 copies. ISBN 0-930901-29-0

118.	**Margaret Johnson,** *A Visit to the Cities of Cheese* (prose poem). 40 pp. Text linotyped in 11 pt. Devinne. Designed and printed letterpress on Warren's Olde Style by Pitt Harding. 2-color title page. 6-1/4x9-1/2, saddlestitched, in Strathmore Brigadoon wrappers. 474 copies. Providence, 1985. ISBN 0-930901-37-1

118a.•	Same. 26 lettered and signed copies

119.•	**Jackson Mac Low,** *The Virginia Woolf Poems.* 44 pp. Text linotyped in 12 pt. Palatino. Designed and printed letterpress on Warren's Olde Style by Rosmarie Waldrop, with title and 4 half titles in 2 colors. Offset cover by Keith Waldrop. 6x9, smyth-sewn paperback. 900 copies. Providence, 1985. ISBN 0-930901-28-2

119a.	Same. Cloth. 100 numbered & signed copies. ISBN 0-930901-27-4

120.	**Barry Schwabsky,** *Fate/Seen in the Dark* (2 poems). 24 pp. Text linotyped in 11 pt. Devinne. Designed and printed letterpress on Warren's Olde Style by Rosmarie Waldrop. 2 colors through-out. 5x9-1/2, saddlestitched, in Strathmore wrappers. 474 copies. Providence, 1985. ISBN 0-930901-34-7

120a.•	Same. 26 lettered and signed copies.

121.• **Gail Sher**, *Broke Aide* (prose). 80 pp. Text linotyped in 11 pt. Devinne. Designed and printed letterpress on Warren's Olde Style by Rosmarie Waldrop, with title and 2 half titles in 2 colors. Offset cover by Keith Waldrop. 5x7-1/4, smyth-sewn paperback. 950 copies. Providence, 1985. ISBN 0-930901-36-3

121a.• Same. Cloth. 50 numbered & signed copies. ISBN 0-930901-35-5

122. **Ron Silliman,** *Paradise* (prose poem). 64 pp. Text linotyped in 12 pt. Palatino. Designed and printed letterpress on Warren's Olde Style by Rosmarie Waldrop, with title and half title in 2 colors. Offset cover by Linda Lutes. 5x7-1/4, smyth-sewn paperback. 900 copies. Providence, 1985. ISBN 0-930901-32-0

122a. Same. Cloth. 100 numbered & signed copies. ISBN 0-930901-31-2

123.• **Joseph Simas,** *Entire Days* (poem). 36 pp. Text linotyped in 12 pt. Palatino. Designed and printed letterpress on Warren's Olde Style by Pitt Harding. 2-color title and half titles. 7x8, saddlestitched, in Artemis wrappers. 724 copies. Providence, 1985. ISBN 0-930901-33-9

123a• Same. 26 lettered & signed copies.

124. **Gil Ott**, *Within Range* (poems & prose). 24 pp. Text linotyped in 11 pt. Caledonia. Designed and printed letterpress on Warren's Olde Style by Rosmarie Waldrop. 2 colors throughout. 6-1/4x9-1/2, saddlestitched, in Strathmore Text and Artemis wrappers. 474 copies. Providence, 1986. ISBN 0-930901-38-x

124a.• Same. 26 lettered & signed copies.

125. **Craig Watson,** *Discipline* (poem). 20 pp. Text linotyped in 11 pt. Devinne. Designed and printed letterpress on Warren's Olde Style by Rosmarie Waldrop. 2 colors throughout. 6-1/4x9-1/2, saddle-stitched, in Strathmore Grandee and Tweedweave wrappers. 474 copies. Providence, 1986. ISBN 0-930901-43-6

125a.• Same. 26 lettered & signed copies.

126.• **Barbara Einzig**, *Life Moves Outside* (short prose). 64 pp. Text linotyped in 10 pt. Palatino. Designed and printed letterpress on Warren's Olde Style by Rosmarie Waldrop, with title and half titles in 2 colors. The offset cover reproduces a photocollage by Phillip Galgiani. 5x7-1/4, smyth-sewn original paperback. 1200 copies. Providence, 1987. ISBN 0-930901-42-8

126a.• Same. 50 numbered and signed copies. ISBN 0-930901-41-x

127.• **Peter Gurnis**, *The Body of Liberties* (poem). 32 pp. Text linotyped in 11 pt. Caledonia. Designed and printed letter-press on Warren's Olde Style by Rosmarie Waldrop. 2 colors throughout. 6-1/4x9-1/2, saddlestitched, in Artemis wrappers. 474 copies. Providence, 1987. ISBN 0-930901-45-2

127a.• Same. 26 lettered & signed copies.

128. **Elizabeth Robinson,** *My Name Happens Also* (poems). 32 pp. Text linotyped in 11 pt. Caledonia. Designed and printed letterpress on Warren's Olde Style by Rosmarie Waldrop. Cover by Keith Waldrop. 6-1/4x9-1/2, saddle-stitched, in Artemis wrappers. 474 copies. Providence, 1987. ISBN 0-930901-44-4

128a.• Same. 26 lettered & signed copies.

129.   **Pat Smith,** *Hour History* (prose & poem). 40 pp. Text linotyped in 11 pt. Caldonia. Designed and printed letterpress on Warren's Olde Style by Rosmarie Waldrop. 2 colors throughout. 6-1/4x9-1/2, saddlestitched, in Cortlea wrappers. 474 copies. Providence, 1987. ISBN 0-930901-39-8

129a.• Same. 26 lettered & signed copies.

130.   **Robert Creeley,** *The Company* (poems). 52 pp. Text linotyped in 10 pt. Palatino. Designed and printed letterpress on Warren's Olde Style by Rosmarie Waldrop. Two colors throughout. Offset cover by Keith Waldrop. 6x6, smyth-sewn original paperback. 800 copies. Providence, 1988. ISBN 0-930901-56-8

130a.   Same. 50 numbered & signed copies. ISBN 0-930901-58-4

131.•   **Laura Chester,** *Free Rein* (poems). 72 pp. Text linotyped in 12 pt. Palatino. Designed and printed letterpress on Warren's Olde Style by Rosmarie Waldrop, with title and half titles in 2 colors. The offset cover reproduces a photograph by B. A. King. 6x9, smyth-sewn original paperback. 1000 copies. Providence, 1988. ISBN 0-930901-54-1

131a.• Same. 50 numbered and signed copies. ISBN 0-930901-55-x

132.•   **Lissa McLaughlin,** *Troubled by His Complexion* (stories). 128 pp. Text linotyped in 10 pt. Palatino, with Jensen and Caslon Oldstyle titles. Designed and printed letterpress on Warren's Olde Style by Rosmarie Waldrop, with the title page in 2 colors. The offset cover reproduces an etching by Leslie Bostrom. 5x7-1/4, smyth-sewn original paperback. 1500 copies. Providence, 1988. ISBN 0-930901-52-5

132a.• Same. 50 numbered & signed copies. ISBN 0-930901-53-3

133.•   **Craig Watson,** *After Calculus* (4 poems). 72 pp. Text linotyped in 11 pt. Devinne. Designed and printed letterpress on Warren's Olde Style by Rosmarie Waldrop, with title and half titles in 2 colors. Offset cover by Keith Waldrop. 6x9, smyth-sewn original paperback. 1000 copies. Providence, 1988. ISBN 0-930901-40-1

133a.• Same. 50 numbered & signed copies. ISBN 0-930901-46-0

134.•   **Dallas Wiebe,** *Going to the Mountain* (stories). 192 pp. Text linotyped in 10 pt. Palatino. Designed and printed letterpress on Warren's Olde Style by Rosmarie Waldrop, with the title page in 2 colors. Initials and offset cover by Keith Waldrop, using a detail from Richard Dadd's "The Fairy Feller's Master Stroke." 5x7-1/4, smyth-sewn original paperback. 2000 copies. Providence, 1988. ISBN 0-930901-49-5

134a.• Same. 50 numbered & signed copies. ISBN 0-930901-50-9

135.   **John Hawkes,** *Island Fire* (story). 13 pp. Handset in 18 pt., 24 pt. and 36 pt. Lutetia, designed & printed letterpress by Keith Waldrop. 2 colors. 5-3/4x8-3/4, Ticonderoga Text, saddlestitched in Strathmore wrappers. 500 copies. Providence, 1988. ISBN 0-930901-59-2

135a.   Same. Printed on Barcham Green Charter Oak, handsewn into Fabriano wrappers. 26 lettered & signed copies. ISBN 0-930901-60-6

136.• **Tina Darragh,** *Striking Resemblance* (4 poems). 64 pp. Text linotyped in 10 pt. Palatino. Designed and printed letterpress on Mohawk Vellum by Rosmarie Waldrop, with title and half titles in 2 colors. Offset cover by Keith Waldrop. 6x9, smyth-sewn original paperback. 1000 copies. Providence, 1989. ISBN 0-930901-64-9

136a.• Same. 50 numbered & signed copies. ISBN 0-930901-65-7

137.• **Harry Mathews,** *Out of Bounds* (poem sequence). 28 pp. Text linotyped in 10 pt. Palatino. Designed and printed letterpress on Warren's Olde Style and Murray Hill Offset by Rosmarie Waldrop. 2 colors throughout. Offset cover by Linda Lutes. 7x5, saddlestitched. 724 copies. Providence, 1989. ISBN 0-930901-61-4

137a. Same. Printed on Barcham Green Charter Oak, handsewn. ISBN 0-930901-62-2

138. **Jena Osman,** *Twelve Parts of Her* (poem sequence). 20 pp. Text linotyped in 10 pt. Palatino. Designed and printed letter-press on Warren's Olde Style by Rosmarie Waldrop. 2 colors throughout. 6-1/4x9-1/2, saddlestitched, in Cortlea, Strathmore and Tweedweave wrappers. 500 copies. Providence, 1989. ISBN 0-930901-63-0

138a.• Same. 26 lettered & signed copies.

139.• **Walter Abish,** *99: The New Meaning* (collage texts). With a cover and 5 additional photographs by Cecile Abish. 112 pp. Text computer typeset in Century Schoolbook. Designed by Keith and Rosmarie Waldrop. Printed offset on Glatfelter and smyth-sewn by Thomson-Shore. 5-1/2x8-1/2. 2500 paperbacks. Providence, 1990. ISBN 930901-66-5

139a.• Same. Cloth. 450 copies. ISBN 930901-67-3

139b.• Same. Signed cloth. 50 copies. ISBN 930901-68-1

140. **Lew Daly,** *e. dickinson on a sleepwalk with the alphabet prowling around her* (poem for two voices). 20 pp. Text handset in 14 pt. Lutetia and printed letterpress on Warren's Olde Style by Keith Waldrop. 2 color title page. 9x4-1/2, saddlestitched into Artemis Cover. 450 copies. Providence, 1990. ISBN 0-930901-69-x

140a.• Same. 50 numbered & signed copies.

141. **Forrest Gander,** *Eggplants and Lotus Root* (poem sequence). 36 pp. Text linotyped in 11 pt. Caledonia, with Cheltenham titles. Designed and printed letterpress on Warren's Olde Style by Rosmarie Waldrop. Cover by Pam Rehm. 2 color title and half titles. 6-1/4x9-1/2, saddlestitched, in Strathmore wrappers. 474 copies. Providence, 1991. ISBN 0-930901-78-9

141a. Same. 26 lettered & signed copies.

142.• **Julie Kalendek,** *The Fundamental Difference* (poems). 40 pp. Text linotyped in 11 pt. Caledonia, with titles in Caslon Oldstyle. Designed and printed letterpress on Warren's Olde Style by Rosmarie Waldrop. Cover by Keith Waldrop. 2 color title and half titles. 6-1/4x9-1/2, saddlestitched, in Strathmore wrappers. 474 copies. Providence, 1991. ISBN 0-930901-79-7

142a.• Same. 26 lettered & signed copies.

143.• **Tom Mandel**, *Realism* (prose and verse). 80 pp. Text computer typeset in 11 pt. Palatino. Designed by the author. Printed offset on 60 lb. Glatfelter and smyth-sewn by Thomson-Shore. Cover by Norma Cole. 6x9, original paperback. 950 copies. Providence, 1991. ISBN 0-930901-70-3

143a.• Same. 50 numbered & signed copies. ISBN 0-930901-71-1

144.• **Gale Nelson**, *stare decisis* (poems). 142 pp. Text computer typeset in 10 pt. Century Schoolbook, with titles in Caslon Oldstyle. Designed by the author and Rosmarie Waldrop. Printed offset on 60 lb. Glatfelter and smyth-sewn by Thomson-Shore. Cover collage by Denis Mizzi. 5-1/2x 8-1/2, original paperback. 950 copies. Providence, 1991. ISBN 0-930901-72-x

144a.• Same. 50 numbered & signed copies. ISBN 0-930901-73-8

145.• **Stephen Rodefer**, *Passing Duration* (prose poems). 64 pp. Text computer typeset in 10 pt. Century Schoolbook, with titles in Boulevard Caps and Caslon Oldstyle. Designed by Rosmarie Waldrop. Printed offset on 60 lb. Glatfelter and smyth-sewn by Thomson-Shore. Cover drawing by Jean Lowe. 5-1/2x9, original paperback. 950 copies. Providence, 1991. ISBN 0-930901-76-2

145a.• Same. 50 numbered & signed copies. ISBN 0-930901-77-0

146.• **Marjorie Welish**, *The Windows Flew Open* (poems). 80 pp. Text computer typeset in 10 pt. Century Schoolbook. Designed by Rosmarie Waldrop. Printed offset on 60 lb. Glatfelter and smyth-sewn by Thomson-Shore. The cover design by the author uses a drawing by Robert Barry. 6x9, original paperback. 1450 copies. Providence, 1991. ISBN 0-930901-74-6

146a.• Same. 50 numbered & signed copies. ISBN 0-930901-75-4

147.• **Barbara Guest**, *The Countess from Minneapolis* (prose & verse). 52 pp. 2nd ed. offset from the letterpress edition [#63], 1976. Printed on 60 lb. Glatfelter by Thomson-Shore. 6x9, smyth-sewn paperback. 1000 copies. Providence 1991. ISBN 0-930900-06-5

148.• **Jean Daive**, *A Lesson in Music*, trans. from the French by Julie Kalendek [*Série d'Ecriture* #6] (poem). 64 pp. Text computer typeset in 10 pt. Century Schoolbook. Designed by Rosmarie Waldrop. Printed offset on 60 lb. Glatfelter and smyth-sewn by Thomson-Shore. Cover photo by the author. 5-1/2x8-1/2. Original paperback. 1000 copies. Providence, 1992. ISSN 0269-0179. ISBN 0-930901-80-0

149.• **Elizabeth MacKiernan**, *Ancestors Maybe* (novel). 160 pp. Text computer typeset in 10 pt. Century Schoolbook, with Optima titles. Designed by Gale Nelson. Cover by Keith Waldrop. Printed offset on 55 lb. Glatfelter and smyth-sewn by McNaughton & Gunn. 5x7. Original paperback. 1450 copies. Providence, 1993. ISBN 0-930901-81-9

149a.• Same. 50 numbered and signed copies. ISBN 0-930901-82-7

150.• **Ray Ragosta**, *Varieties of Religious Experience* (poems). 80 pp. Text computer typeset in 11 pt. Palatino with Bernhard Gothic titles. Designed by the author and Rosmarie Waldrop. Cover by Keith Waldrop. Printed offset on 60 lb.Glatfelter and smyth-sewn by Thomson-Shore. 6x9. Original paperback. 950 copies. Providence 1993. ISBN 0-930900-83-5

150a.• Same. 50 numbered and signed copies. ISBN 0-930901-84-3

151.• **Brita Bergland,** *The Rebirth of the Older Child* (poems). 64 pp. Text computer typeset in 10 pt. Century Schoolbook, with Caslon Oldstyle titles. Designed by Rosmarie Waldrop. Cover by Keith Waldrop. Printed offset on 55 lb. Glatfelter and smyth-sewn by McNaughton & Gunn. 6x9. Original paperback. 1000 copies. Providence, 1993. ISBN 0-930901-85-1

151a.• Same. 50 numbered and signed copies. ISBN 0-930901-86-x

152.• **Pam Rehm,** *The Garment In Which No One Had Slept* (poems). 64 pp. Text computer typeset in 10 pt. Century Schoolbook, with Optima titles. Designed by the author and Rosmarie Waldrop. Printed offset on 60 lb. Glatfelter and smyth-sewn by Thomson-Shore. 6x9. Original paperback. 950 copies. Providence 1993. ISBN 0-930900-87-8

152a.• Same. 50 numbered and signed copies. ISBN 0-930901-88-6

153.• **Claire Needell,** Not A Balancing Act (poems). 64 pp. Text computer typeset in 10 pt. Century Schoolbook, with Caslon Oldstyle titles. Designed by Rosmarie Waldrop. Cover collage by Denis Mizzi. Printed offset on 55 lb. Glatfelter and smyth-sewn by McNaughton & Gunn. . 6x9. Original paperback. 1000 copies. Providence, 1993. ISBN 0-930901-89-4

153a.• Same. 50 numbered and signed copies. ISBN 0-930901-90-8

154.• **Keith & Rosmarie Waldrop,** *Light Travels* (poem). 36 pp. Text linotyped in 11 pt. Caledonia with handset Caslon Oldstyle and Cheltenham titles. Designed and printed letterpress on Warren's Olde Style by Keith Waldrop. 2 colors throughout. 6-1/4x4-3/4, saddlestitched, in Strathmore wrappers. 500 copies. Providence, 1991. ISBN 0-930901-92-4

155. *Série d'Ecriture* #7. Texts by Jacques Roubaud, Pierre Alferi, Esther Tellerman, Jean-Pierre Boyer, Jean Frémon, Dominique Fourcade, Anne Portugal, Jean-Marie Gleize, Anne Talvaz, Olivier Cadiot, James Sacré, Isabelle Hovald, Dominique Grandmont, Emmanuel Hocquard. Translated by David Ball, Norma Cole, Stacy Doris, Paul Green, Tom Mandel, Pam Rehm, Cole Swensen, Keith Waldrop, Rosmarie Waldrop. 96 pp. Text computer typeset in 10 pt. Century Schoolbook with Optima titles. Designed by Rosmarie Waldrop. The cover reproduces a bookmark by Simon Hantaï for *Outrance Utterance* by Dominique Fourcade. Printed offset on Glatfelter and smyth-sewn by McNaughton & Gunn. 8-1/2x5-1/2. Original paperback. 700 copies. Providence, 1993. ISSN 0269-0179. ISBN 0-930901-93-2

156.• **Paol Keineg,** *Boudica*, trans. from the French by Keith Waldrop [*Série d'Ecriture* #8] (poem). 64 pp. Text computer typeset in 10 pt. Century Schoolbook with Optima titles. Designed by Rosmarie Waldrop. Printed offset on 55 lb. Glatfelter and smyth-sewn by McNaughton & Gunn. The cover by Keith Waldrop uses a photo of Thornycroft's statue of Queen Boadicea. 5-1/2x8-1/2. Original paperback. 1000 copies. Providence, 1994. ISSN 0269-0179. ISBN 0-930901-94-0

157.• **Friederike Mayröcker,** *Heiligenanstalt*, trans. from the German by Rosmarie Waldrop [*Dichten=* #1] (4 proses). 96 pp. Text computer typeset in 10 pt. Century Schoolbook. Designed by Rosmarie Waldrop. Printed offset on 55 lb. Glatfelter and smyth-sewn by McNaughton & Gunn. The cover reproduces a score by Chopin. 5-1/2x8-1/2. Original paperback. 1000 copies. Providence, 1994. ISSN 1077-4203. ISBN 0-930901-95-9

158.• **David Miller,** *Stromata* (poems). 64 pp. Text computer typeset in 10 pt. Century Schoolbook, with Optima titles. Designed by Rosmarie Waldrop. Cover by Andrew Bick. Printed offset on 55 lb. Glatfelter and smyth-sewn by McNaughton & Gunn. 6x9. Original paperback. 950 copies. Providence 1995. ISBN 0-930900-96-7

158a.• Same. 50 numbered and signed copies. ISBN 0-930901-97-5

159.• **Brian Schorn,** *Strabismus* (poems). 64 pp. Text computer typeset in 10 pt. Goudy with Akzidenz Grotesk titles. Designed by the author. Printed offset on 55 lb. Glatfelter and smyth-sewn by McNaughton & Gunn. 5-1/2x8-1/2. Original paperback. 950 copies. Providence 1995. ISBN 0-930900-98-3

159a.• Same. 50 numbered and signed copies. ISBN 0-930901-99-1

160. **Cole Swensen,** *Numen* (poems). 64 pp. Text computer typeset in 10 pt. Century Schoolbook. Designed by Rosmarie Waldrop. The cover by Keith Waldrop uses a photo from Frank Gilbreth's 1916 *Fatigue Study: The Elimination of Humanity's Greatest Unnecessary Waste.* Printed offset on 55 lb. Glatfelter and smyth-sewn by McNaughton & Gunn. 6x9. Original paperback. 950 copies. Providence 1995. ISBN 1-886224-00-5

160a.• Same. 50 numbered and signed copies. ISBN 1-886224-01-3

161.• **Dallas Wiebe,** *Skyblue's Essays* (fictions). 160 pp. Text computer typeset in 10 pt. Century Schoolbook. Designed by Rosmarie Waldrop. Cover photos by Bill Manrick and Jon Hughes. Printed offset on 55 lb. Glatfelter and smyth-sewn by McNaughton & Gunn. 5x7. Original paperback. 1000 copies. Providence 1995. ISBN 1-886224-02-1

161a.• Same. 50 numbered and signed copies. ISBN 1-886224-03-x

162.• **Damon Krukowski,** *5000 Musical Terms* (poems). 28 pp. Text linotyped in 10 pt. Palatino with handset 18 pt. Bernhard Gothic Medium titles. Designed and printed letterpress on Warren's Olde Style by Rosmarie Waldrop. Cover by Keith Waldrop. 2 color titlepage. 6-1/4x9-1/2, saddlestitched, in Artemis wrappers. 500 copies. Providence, 1995. ISBN 1-886224-04-8

162a.• Same. 26 numbered and signed copies. ISBN 1-886224-05-6

163.• **Elke Erb,** *Mountains in Berlin,* selected and trans. from the German by Rosmarie Waldrop [*Dichten=* #2] (poems). 96 pp. Text computer typeset in 10 pt. Century Schoolbook. Designed by Rosmarie Waldrop. Printed offset on 55 lb. Glatfelter and smyth-sewn by McNaughton & Gunn. The cover reproduces an etching by Carlfriedrich Claus. 5-1/2x8-1/2. Original paperback. 1000 copies. Providence, 1995. ISSN 1077-4203. ISBN 1-886224-06-4

164.• **Marcel Cohen,** *The Peacock Emperor Moth,* trans. from the French by Cid Corman [*Série d'Ecriture* #9] (stories). 112 pp. Text computer typeset in 10 pt. Palatino. Designed by Rosmarie Waldrop. Printed offset on 55 lb. Glatfelter and smyth-sewn by McNaughton & Gunn. The cover reproduces "Portrait" by Antonio Saura. 5-1/2x8-1/2. Original paperback. 1000 copies. Providence, 1995. ISSN 0269-0179. ISBN 1-886224-07-2

165.• **Claude Royet-Journoud**, *i.e.*, trans. from the French by Keith Waldrop [*Série d'Ecriture* Supplement #1] (poem). 20 pp. Text computer typeset in 10 pt. Century Schoolbook. Designed by Rosmarie Waldrop. Cover by Keith Waldrop. Printed offset on 60 lb. Offset and saddle-stitched by Jo-Art. 5-1/2x8-1/2. 750 copies. Providence, 1995. ISSN 0269-0179. ISBN 1-886224-08-0

166. **Paul Auster**, *Why Write?* (essays). 64 pp. Text computer typeset in 10 pt. Palatino. Designed by Rosmarie Waldrop. Printed offset on 55 lb. Glatfelter and smyth-sewn by McNaughton & Gunn. 5x7. 2000 paperbacks. Providence, 1996. ISBN 1-886224-14-5

166a. Same. Cloth. 450 copies. ISBN 1-886224-15-3

166b. Same. Signed cloth. 50 copies. ISBN 1-886224-16-1

167.• **Lisa Jarnot**, *Some Other Kind of Mission* (poems). 112pp. Text computer typeset in 10 pt. Palatino. Designed by Rosmarie Waldrop. Printed offset on 55 lb. Glatfelter and smyth-sewn by McNaughton & Gunn. The cover by the author reproduces an etching by Bruce Kurland. 6x9. Original paperback. 950 copies. Providence, 1996. ISBN 1-886224-12-9

167a.• Same. 50 numbered and signed copies. ISBN 1-886224-13-7

168.• **Jessica Lowenthal**, *as if in turning* (poems). 28 pp. Text linotyped in 11 pt. Caledonia with handset Caslon Old Style/Boulevard Caps titles. Designed and printed letterpress on Mohawk Vellum by Rosmarie Waldrop. Cover by Keith Waldrop. 2 colors throughout. 6-1/4x9-1/2, saddlestitched, in Artemis wrappers. 500 copies. Providence, 1996. ISBN 1-886224-17-x

168a.• Same. 26 numbered and signed copies. ISBN 1-886224-18-8

169. **Mark McMorris**, *Moth-Wings*, 40 pp. Text linotyped in 11 pt. Caledonia with handset Lutetia and Berthold Post Roman Bold titles. Designed and printed letterpress on Mohawk Vellum by Rosmarie Waldrop. Cover by Keith Waldrop. 2 color title and half titles. 6-1/4x9-1/2, saddlestitched, in Artemis wrappers. 500 copies. Providence, 1996. ISBN 1-886224-10-2

169a.• Same. 26 numbered and signed copies. ISBN 1-886224-11-0

170.• **Jacqueline Risset**, *The Translation Begins* (poem). Trans. from the French by Jennifer Moxley [*Série d'Ecriture* #10]. 96 pp. Text computer typeset in 10 pt. Palatino. Designed by Rosmarie Waldrop. Printed offset on 55 lb. Glatfelter and smyth-sewn by McNaughton & Gunn. The cover reproduces a detail from a Greek Krater, courtesy Museum of Fine Arts, Boston. 5-1/2x8-1/2. Original paperback. 1000 copies. Providence, 1996. ISSN 0269-0179. ISBN 1-886224-09-9

171.• **Pascal Quignard**, *Sarx*, trans. from the French by Keith Waldrop [*Série d'Ecriture* Supplement #2] (poem). 40 pp. Text computer typeset in 10 pt. Palatino. Designed by Rosmarie Waldrop. Cover by Keith Waldrop. Printed offset on 60 lb. Offset and saddle-stitched by Jo-Art. 5-1/2x8-1/2. 500 copies. Providence, 1997. ISSN 0269-0179. ISBN 1-886224-20-x

172.• **Alain Veinstein**, *Even a Child*, trans. from the French by Robert Kocik and Rosmarie Waldrop [*Série d'Ecriture* #11] (poems). 64 pp. Text computer typeset in 12 pt. Palatino. Designed by Rosmarie Waldrop. Printed offset on 55 lb. Glatfelter and smyth-sewn by McNaughton & Gunn. Cover by Keith Waldrop. 5-1/2x8-1/2. Original paperback. 750 copies. Providence, 1997. ISSN 0269-0179. ISBN 1-886224-28-5

173.• **Ilma Rakusa,** *Steppe,* translated from the German by Solveig Emerson [Dichten= #3] (stories). 80 pp. Text computer typeset in 10 pt. Palatino. Designed by Rosmarie Waldrop. Printed offset on 55 lb. Glatfelter and smyth-sewn by McNaughton & Gunn. Cover by Keith Waldrop. 5-1/2x8-1/2. Original paperback. 1000 copies. Providence, 1997. ISSN 1077-4203. ISBN 1-886224-27-7

174.• **Sianne Ngai,** *Discredit* (poem). 32 pp. Text linotyped in 9 pt. Palatino with handset Caslon Oldstyle and Anniversary titlepage. Designed and printed letterpress on Mohawk Vellum by Rosmarie Waldrop. Cover by Keith Waldrop. 2 colors. 6-1/4x9-1/2, saddle-stitched, in Artemis wrappers. 474 copies. Providence, 1996. ISBN 1-886224-25-0

174a.• Same. 26 numbered and signed copies. ISBN 1-886224-26-9

175.• **Keith Waldrop,** *Analogies of Escape* (poems). 80 pp. Text computer typeset in 10 pt. Palatino. Designed by Rosmarie Waldrop. Printed offset on 55 lb. Writer's Natural and smyth-sewn by McNaughton & Gunn. Cover by Keith Waldrop. 6x9. Original paperback. 950 copies. Providence, 1997. ISBN 1-886224-29-3

175a.• Same. Numbered & signed. 50 copies. ISBN 1-886224-30-7

176.• **Alison Bundy,** *Duncecap* (stories). 128 pp. Text computer typeset in 10 pt. Palatino. Designed by Rosmarie Waldrop. Printed offset on 55 lb. Writers Natural (an acid-free paper) and smyth-sewn by McNaughton & Gunn. 5x7. Original paperback. 950 copies. Providence, 1998. ISBN 1-886224-23-4

176a.• Same. 50 numbered & signed copies. ISBN 1-886224-24-2

177.• **Peter Gizzi,** *Artificial Heart* (poems). 96 pp. Text computer typeset in 10.5 pt. Janson Text. Designed by Brian Schorn. Printed offset on 55 lb. Glatfelter and smyth-sewn by McNaughton & Gunn. The cover by Brian Schorn uses a photograph by Tina Modotti. 6x8-1/2. Original paperback. 950 copies. Providence, 1998. ISBN 1-886224-21-8

177a.• Same. 50 numbered and signed copies. ISBN 1-886224-22-6

178.• **Xue Di,** *Heart Into Soil* (poems). Trans. from the Chinese by Keith Waldrop with Wang Ping, Iona Crook, Janet Tan and Hil Anderson. 96 pp. Text computer typeset in 10 pt. Palatino. Designed by Rosmarie Waldrop. Printed offset on 55 lb. Writers Natural (an acid-free paper) and smyth-sewn by McNaughton & Gunn. The cover by Keith Waldrop uses a photo of the author by John Foraste. 6x9. Original paperback. 1000 copies. Co-production with Lost Roads. Providence/Barrington, 1998. ISBN 1-886224-32-3

179.• **Anne-Marie Albiach,** *A Geometry,* trans. from the French by Keith & Rosmarie Waldrop [*Série d'Ecriture* Supplement #3] (poems). 28 pp. Text computer typeset in 10 pt. Palatino. Designed by Rosmarie Waldrop. Cover by Keith Waldrop. Printed offset on 60 lb. Offset and saddle-stitched by Jo-Art. 5-1/2x8-1/2. 750 copies. Providence, 1998. ISSN 0269-0179. ISBN 1-886224-08-0

180.• **Emmanuel Hocquard**, *A Test of Solitude*, trans. from the French by Rosmarie Waldrop [*Série d'Ecriture* #12] (sonnets). 72 pp. Text computer typeset in 10 pt. Palatino. Designed by Rosmarie Waldrop. Printed offset on 55 lb. Writers Natural (an acid-free paper) and smyth-sewn by McNaughton & Gunn. The cover by Keith Waldrop uses a photograph by Jean Khalfa. 5-1/2x8-1/2. Original paperback. 1000 copies. Providence, 2000. ISSN 0269-0179. ISBN 1-886224-331

181.• **Ernst Jandl**, *reft and light.*, ed. Rosmarie Waldrop, with various translators [*Dichten=* #4] (poems). 112 pp. Text computer typeset in 10 pt. Palatino and Courier. Designed by Rosmarie Waldrop. Printed offset on 55 lb. Writers Natural (an acidfree paper) and smyth-sewn by McNaughton & Gunn. Cover by Keith Waldrop. 5-1/2x8-1/2. 1000 Original paperback. Providence, 2000. ISSN 1077-4203. ISBN 1-886224-34-x

182.• **Gale Nelson**, *ceteris paribus* (poems). 128 pp. Text computer typeset in 9.75 pt. Palatino, New York, Times New Roman and Verdana. Designed by Gale Nelson. Printed offset on 55 lb. Writers Natural and smyth-sewn by McNaughton & Gunn. The cover by the author uses two collages by Keith Waldrop. 5-1/2x8-1/2. Original paperback. 950 copies. Providence, 2000. ISBN 1-886224-37-4

182a.• Same. 50 numbered and signed copies. ISBN 1-886224-38-2

183.• **Jane Unrue**, *The House* (prose). 64 pp. Text computer typeset in 10 pt. Palatino. Designed by Rosmarie Waldrop. Printed offset on 55 lb. Writers Natural and smyth-sewn by McNaughton & Gunn. Cover by Keith Waldrop. 5x7. Original paperback. 950 copies. Providence, 2000. ISBN 1-886224-35-8

183a.• Same. 50 numbered and signed copies. ISBN 1-886224-36-6

184.• **Norma Cole**, ed./trans., *Crosscut Universe: Writing on Writing from France.* [*Série d'Ecriture* #13/14]. 160 pp. Text computer typeset in 10 pt. Palatino. Designed by Rosmarie Waldrop. Printed offset on 55 lb. Writers Natural and smyth-sewn by McNaughton & Gunn. The cover uses a drawing by Raquel. 5-1/2x8-1/2. Original paperback. 2000 copies. Providence, 2000. ISSN 0269-0179. ISBN 1-886224-39-0

185.• **Susan Gevirtz**, *Hourglass Transcripts* (poems). 72 pp. Text computer typeset in 10 pt. Palatino with Zapf Chancery Initials. Split lines courtesy of David Delp. Designed by Rosmarie Waldrop. Printed offset on 55 lb. Writers Natural and smyth-sewn by NcNaughton & Gunn. Cover by Keith Waldrop. 6x9. Original paperback. 700 copies. Providence, 2001. ISBN 1-886224-40-4

185a.• Same. 50 numbered and signed copies. ISBN 1-886224-41-2

186.• **Jennifer Martenson**, *Xq28[1]* (poem). 20 pp. Text computer typeset in 9 pt. Palatino with Dom Casual titles. Designed by Rosmarie Waldrop and the author. Printed offset on 55 lb. Writers Natural and saddlestitched by Allegra Print and Imaging in Providence, RI. Cover by Keith Waldrop. 5-1/2x8-1/2. 500 copies. Providence, 2001. ISBN 1-886224-42-0

186a.• Same. 26 lettered and signed copies. ISBN 1-886224-43-9

187.• **Oskar Pastior,** *Many Glove Compartment*s (selected poems). Translated from the German by Harry Mathews, Christopher Middleton, Rosmarie Waldrop (with a guest appearance by John Yau). [*Dichten=* #5]. 120 pp. Text computer typeset in 10 pt. Palatino. Designed by Rosmarie Waldrop. Printed offset on 55 lb. Writers Natural and smyth-sewn by McNaughton & Gunn. Cover by Keith Waldrop. 5-1/2x8-1/2. Original paperback. 1000 copies. Providence, 2001. ISSN 1077-4203. ISBN 1-886224-44-7

188.• **Pascal Quignard,** *On Wooden Tablets: Apronenia Avitia* (novel). Translated from the French by Bruce X. [*Série d'Ecriture* #15]. 112 pp. Text computer typeset in 10 pt. Palatino. Designed by Rosmarie Waldrop. Printed offset on 55 lb. Writers Natural and smyth-sewn by McNaughton & Gunn. Cover by Keith Waldrop. 5-1/2x8-1/2. Original paperback. 1000 copies. Providence, 2001. ISSN 0269-0179. ISBN 1-886224-45-5

This book was designed and computer typeset in 10 pt. Palatino (with Zapf Chancery titles) by Rosmarie Waldrop. Printed on 55 lb. Writers' Natural (an acid-free paper), smyth-sewn and glued into paper covers by McNaughton & Gunn in Saline, Michigan. The cover is by Keith Waldrop. There are 1500 copies.